"All I have needed Thy hand hath provided.
Great is Thy faithfulness, Lord unto me."

Thomas O. Chisholm

Miriam Jones Bradley

All I Have Needed
a Legacy for Life

All I Have Needed
a Legacy for Life

MIRIAM JONES BRADLEY

with C. Bruce Bradley

Ambassador International
GREENVILLE, SOUTH CAROLINA & BELFAST, NORTHERN IRELAND

www.ambassador-international.com

ALL I HAVE NEEDED—A LEGACY FOR LIFE

Printed in the United States of America

ISBN: 978-1-62020-210-4
eISBN: 978-1-62020-308-8

All Scripture quotations, unless otherwise indicated, are taken from the King James Version.

Cover design: Hannah Stanley
Typesetting: Matthew Mulder
E-book conversion: Anna Riebe

AMBASSADOR INTERNATIONAL
Emerald House
427 Wade Hampton Blvd.
Greenville, SC 29609, USA
www.ambassador-international.com

AMBASSADOR BOOKS
The Mount
2 Woodstock Link
Belfast, BT6 8DD, Northern Ireland, UK
www.ambassadormedia.co.uk

The colophon is a trademark of Ambassador

This book is dedicated to my daddy—Marvin Burell Jones—
who more than anyone else gave me the tools
I needed to become who I am today. I love you, Daddy.

Dedication:

IN GRATITUDE TO THOSE WHO came before us for leaving such a clear path.

Some of them have gone on ahead:

Grandparents: George Lee Jones, Mildred Lenore Jones, F.W. McKnight, Elnora May McKnight, Carroll A. Onstott, Naomi Stoddard Onstott, Elizabeth McGee Onstott, Clarence Bradley, Sarah Middleton Bradley, Corrie Jackson Hipp, Hy Mizruchy

Parents: Calvin Archie Bradley, Olivia Hipp Bradley, Elnora Ann McKnight Jones

We are thankful that some are still with us, sharing their wisdom every chance they get: Marvin Burell Jones, Dortha Lennae Onstott Jones, Grandma Babs Mizruchy, and all of our aunts and uncles.

Acknowledgements:

THANK YOU TO MY PARENTS for reading the manuscript and offering valuable help in making sure the facts are correct. Also, I could not do this without my husband's excellent editorial assistance. He's the one who makes me a much better writer. I also want to thank the readers of my blog who encouraged me to put this book together. Thank you in advance to my family for once again letting me put our stories out there for everybody to see! (I know, I know! I didn't ask, did I?) Finally, for all who prayed for us as we worked on this project, thank you! HE answered. Any errors in this book are mine, all mine!

Contents

SECTION 1

A Legacy of Spirit-Filled Living

SECTION 6

Legacy of Affirmation

SECTION 7

Legacy of Common Sense

Preface:

DURING DECEMBER OF 1997 AND January of 1998, three of my grandparents died. I began to think in earnest of my grandparents and parents. None of them were wealthy people by any stretch of the imagination, so they did not leave me riches. But the legacy they did leave was far more valuable: a legacy of godly lives.

Webster defines a legacy as "something coming from an ancestor or predecessor." Colossians 3:17 says, *Whatsoever ye do in word or deed, do all in the name of the Lord Jesus.* Also, in 1 Timothy 4:12 we are told to *be an example of the believers, in word, in conversation, in charity, in spirit, in faith, and in purity.*

As I look at my life and how it has been molded by these people, I find that theirs has truly been a legacy for life. This legacy has been one that encompassed as many different areas as they possessed different personalities and gifts. Therefore, my legacy isn't just one of word or deed. It doesn't just cover conversation or charity, faith or purity, but is a legacy of completeness. All I have needed has been provided.

Nearly every day I'm reminded of something from my childhood. Usually it's a lesson I learned from one of my grandparents or parents. I like writing them down. This is a collection of those stories written over several years. The pieces are arranged topically rather than chronologically.

A Legacy Should Not Be Wasted

I AM IMPRESSIONABLE. I ADMIT it.

For instance, when I watch the movies made from Jane Austen books, I have to make a pot of tea. When I watch *You've Got Mail*, I need a cappuccino.

Every morning I choose a coffee mug based solely on my feelings. I stand in front of my wall of mugs and say to myself, "Which one do I feel like using today?" Then, depending on my emotions, who I am missing, what the weather is like, or what day of the week it is, I pick a mug.

Like I said, I'm impressionable.

For this reason—if no other—I am exceedingly grateful for my upbringing. We've all seen those impressionable souls who can't decide what they believe. They can't make right choices. They always seem to be following the wrong guidance. I really believe I have that potential in me, considering my impressionability factor.

So, what made the difference?

I have been given—by God, no doubt—a precious and valuable gift. It came packaged in my parents and grandparents.

For this impressionable child, nothing was more valuable than a world filled to the brim with mature, loving, consistent, godly examples of the fruit of the Spirit. I'm not exaggerating here, folks. My parents and grandparents taught me everything I need to know to succeed in life. I have been wrapped in a cocoon of positive influences.

I have seen—lived out in full color—self-discipline, the value of hard work, a vibrant prayer life, patience, forgiveness, wonderful marriages, meekness, goodness, faith, moral excellence, determination, humor, and the list could go on and on.

My spirit was overwhelmed yesterday as I drove to work. Why me? Why did God bless me with this amazing life? So many people struggle through life, overcoming their surroundings, and yet I am given this amazing opportunity. Why? I'm reminded of a Bible principle my daddy taught me. With great opportunity comes great responsibility.

My prayer is that I would seek to use the opportunities God gives me to make the best use of this legacy. It must not be wasted.

The lines have fallen to me in pleasant places, yea I have a goodly heritage (Psalm 16:6).

Section 1

A Legacy of Spirit-Filled Living

Good Ears . . . Great Listener

IF I TOLD GRANDMA JONES that I miss her today, I wonder, would she hear me up there in heaven? Grandma Jones had great hearing. Seriously. It was a joke in our family, but it was a joke based on hard fact. If you wanted to say something she wouldn't hear, you needed to go to the back of the house, down the stairs, huddle in the basement, and whisper. Softly!

When you came back upstairs, she would give you "that look," the one that told you she knew what you were up to. I always wondered if she could truly hear us whispering down there.

She wasn't just a good "hearer" but also an awesome listener. She was a woman of above average intelligence, but she didn't flaunt it. She listened. She listened to Grandpa's stories. She listened to her sister's stories. She listened to her children's stories, then to her grandchildren's stories. Every once in a while, in the midst of the conversation, she would say something. It was always succinct, short and sweet, and right on the money. If Grandma spoke, it was worth listening to.

One of the main things that made Grandma such a good listener was her ability to keep things to herself. She was known for never saying a bad thing about anyone. So, all of those things she heard as conversations swirled around her, she kept to herself. If she clamped her mouth shut in the middle of a conversation, you knew. She knew something, and she wasn't letting it cross her lips.

Another thing that made Grandma such a great listener was the Holy Spirit. When she trusted Christ, He enabled her to hold her tongue even beyond her normal ability. Wow!

There are many, many times I wish God had given me a bit more of that gene. But then I remember: I have the same Holy Spirit. So, while I may not have the natural bent toward listening that Grandma had, I do have the same power that enabled her to practice her listening skills.

I'm sure that today in heaven, Grandma is not focusing on what is being said down here in the basement. She is probably sitting at the feet of Jesus, listening to Him. Maybe He will tell her how much she is missed.

Treasures on a Tablecloth

"Don't put your fingers on the piano; the oil will ruin the wood."
~ Grandma McKnight

THE OTHER MORNING, MY HUSBAND dropped a blueberry from his pancake onto the tablecloth.

"Oh, no, it's going to stain," he lamented.

I just smiled.

The fact that there will be a new stain on my tablecloth doesn't bother me one bit. Not on this tablecloth. For me it will simply be another bit of history, right there for us to see.

This particular tablecloth is rather old. It belonged to my mother. It is cotton with red and blue flowers on it. It's bright and cheerful. It has a small child's handprints all over it.

Yep, that's right. Smack in the middle of the tablecloth are two little hand prints. It looks like a child with some kind of greasy, inky something on his hands climbed up on the table and put his hands smack in the middle of the tablecloth.

I love the little hand prints. I don't know whose they are. I think they could be my brother's, but I have no proof of that. They could just as easily be mine.

At any rate, I like to see them there. I like the fact that my mother kept the tablecloth, even though it was "ruined." It reminds me that people are more important than things.

And now, here we are some forty years later, adding more stains. I wonder if anyone will ever question where that blueberry stain came from? Will they see the tablecloth as ruined? Or, will they, like me, see it as the precious memory of a Saturday morning breakfast with the man I love? I hope they see love.

Two Proverbs 31 Ladies

WHEN I WAS A LITTLE girl, my two grandmas intrigued me. They were both godly women. They loved their husbands and children. The world is a better place because they were here.

They were as different as night and day.

Once I grew into a young woman, I continued to look at my grandmas and wonder. Which was more spiritual? Which one should I pattern my life after? This questioning coincided with a stage I went through where I was trying really hard to be a Proverbs 31 woman. We do this as women. We read the chapter over and over. We dissect and memorize. We analyze and evaluate. We compare.

We aren't supposed to compare.

See, I shouldn't compare my grandmothers. They were very different people. They were born in different places, to different parents, with different personalities. God had different purposes for their lives.

Grandma Jones was born to a farm couple in Nebraska. She spent her entire life in Nebraska. She went as far in school as she could—through the ninth grade—a year farther than most of her peers. She rode to town in a car without a top so she could go to ninth grade. She loved to learn. She was very intelligent, especially excelling in mental arithmetic. She told me she would have enjoyed being a bookkeeper.

She was a behind-the-scenes sort of person. She was quiet, witty, and gentle of spirit. At eighteen, she married a cowboy and stood at his side through thick and thin. She was an awesome cook, seamstress, and keeper of the house. When they were first married, she lived in a sod house without complaint. She did without so her children could have what they needed. At the time of her death, she had 113 direct descendants. She appeared to love everyone equally. She was a good friend. She taught Sunday school to children. She loved babies. She matter-of-factly did her daily tasks over and over again, all to the glory of God. She never said a bad word about anyone, ever.

Grandma McKnight was born to city people. Her parents were musical. She and her daddy sang and made music every chance they got. She was outgoing and vibrant. She was extremely talented musically and taught piano and organ.

She married a preacher boy. They lived in eight different states, from California to Georgia. She traveled. She was a gifted speaker and a great pastor's wife. She was a prayer warrior. She loved to disciple young women and gave me some of her notes from ladies' conferences.

When we went to her house, she always had a project for us to do or verses to learn. On one visit, she made me learn Philippians 2 so "if you ever are asked to speak at the last minute, you will have something to say." She was a mover and shaker with a gift of management, but she also loved her husband and children and made her home a priority.

I learned a lot from these two women, but the most important thing I learned is this. I need to be myself. I need to use the gifts

God gave me. I don't need to try to be someone else, not even one of my godly grandmas. If I use the talents and gifts God has given me the way He expects, I will be a Proverbs 31 lady, and I won't even have to try.

> *"Memorize Philippians 2:5-11 and if you are ever asked to speak, you will have something to say!"*
>
> ~ Grandma McKnight

Public Displays of Affection ... or Not

MY DAD'S PARENTS WERE RANCH people. They grew up in Nebraska during simpler times when the work was hard and there weren't many frills. They lived in a sod house (where Daddy was born), and they lost everything during the Depression. When people talked about the "good old days," Grandma would say, "They weren't so good." They were loving but not demonstrative, at least not toward each other in front of others. That wasn't their way.

When Grandpa was about ninety, he developed a lump on his neck. He ignored it as it got bigger and bigger. After all, he was ninety. He didn't expect to live forever. One day it started causing trouble with his breathing, so they took him to the hospital, rushed him sixty-five miles from Broken Bow to Kearney, Nebraska. That lump had to be removed.

The morning of surgery, the staff came in to take Grandpa to the procedure and told Grandma, "You can kiss him goodbye if you want." To my parents' amazement and delight, she did. It wouldn't be considered a romantic moment by today's standards, but it certainly impressed Daddy. After all, at age sixty-five he was watching—for the first time—his parents kiss.

During the preparations for surgery, Grandpa's IV came apart,

29

and he bled some. He bled enough that the doctors decided they should take him back to his room and check his heart before doing surgery. After all, he was ninety. Once he was cleared for surgery, Grandma had her chance again, and she went for it.

"Twice," Daddy said. "I saw them kiss twice!" The look on his face when he was telling us was priceless. It was pure delight and comfort. Proof of what we all knew. They loved. (As if one hundred direct descendants and sixty-five years of marriage wasn't enough proof.)

A couple of years later, Grandpa was hospitalized with a mild heart attack. It was caused, it turned out, by prostate cancer, and he was dying. Grandma, herself well into her 80s, couldn't care for him at home, so they put him in the nursing home attached to the hospital. During the next six weeks, Grandma went up every day to eat lunch with him . . . well, at least until she figured out that he wasn't eating when she was there in hopes she would take pity on him and take him home. She certainly wanted him home, but it was impossible, so she started going after lunch and sitting with him all afternoon.

Grandpa kept asking to see my youngest niece, who was about six months old, because he hadn't seen her yet. So, my sister and I took the children and drove down to visit for a few days. Grandpa was miserable and in pain, but uncomplaining.

One afternoon, Cheryl brought Grandma to the nursing home to visit. We pushed her wheelchair up close to the bed where they sat in silence, holding hands. He peered at her and asked, "Do you have enough money at the house for food?"

She smiled and assured him, "Yes, George, I have plenty." I understood something that day. Love isn't just about hugs and kisses.

It isn't about telling someone they are beautiful or handsome. It certainly isn't just about romance. Love is about caring and providing. It is about sharing your lives, both the good and the bad.

I wonder, in today's world, where demonstrations of affection are everywhere you look, is it really better? After all, Grandpa and Grandma Jones were married for sixty-seven years. Theirs was a grand love story, and no one who knew them would doubt it for one moment. I sure didn't doubt it that day in the nursing home.

> *"When we were young, there wasn't much divorce. If you didn't like each other one day, you just waited a few days until you did."*
>
> ~ Grandma Jones

My Grandma and Bin Laden – The Words We Choose

"Let your speech be alway with grace, seasoned with salt, that ye may know how ye ought to answer every man."

~ Colossians 4:6

I AM SO GRATEFUL THAT Osama bin Laden was brought to justice. I'm thankful to our wonderful military and the government leaders who made the necessary decisions that led to his death.

I couldn't help but think of Grandma Jones when I heard the news. I think of her every time I hear bin Laden's name.

Grandma was best known for one thing. She kept her peace. If she couldn't think of anything nice to say, she just didn't say anything. She was the epitome of the phrase from Proverbs 31:26 that says "In her tongue is the law of kindness."

The worst thing I ever heard her say about anyone was what she said about bin Laden after 9/11. She tended toward short statements. Short and sweet, generally, but when it wasn't sweet, it got even shorter. What she said about bin Laden that day struck me stronger than any long speech I've heard on the subject.

"That ornery guy."

Three words. That's all she had to say about him. The look

on her face and her tone of voice said more than the words. In her voice was every bit of disregard she could muster. I thought about what she would say now, if she was still alive. I had an imaginary conversation with her. "Grandma, bin Laden was killed."

"Good."

One of my Jones cousins mentioned that her other grandpa was exactly like Grandma. He didn't often say anything negative, either. In fact, the worst thing she ever heard him say was about bin Laden also. He said, "What a dirty dog."

It started me thinking. We are surrounded every day by angry people making angry statements. People spout unkind, hurtful things. I've thought many times how much I wished I was more like Grandma. Imagine what the world would be like if the worst thing we said was "That ornery guy" or "What a dirty dog." What if we saved the truly bad phrases for the people who deserved them?

What if we took a page from Grandma Jones' and Granddad Edington's book? What if . . .

She openeth her mouth with wisdom; and in her tongue is the law of kindness (Proverbs 31:26).

Red Geraniums

Life did not bring me silken gowns,
Nor jewels for my hair,
Nor signs of gabled foreign towns
In distant countries fair,
But I can glimpse, beyond my pane, a green and friendly hill,
And red geraniums aflame upon my window sill.

The brambled cares of everyday,
The tiny humdrum things,
May bind my feet when they would stray,
But still my heart has wings
While red geraniums are bloomed against my window glass,
And low above my green-sweet hill the gypsy wind-clouds pass.

And if my dreaming ne'er come true,
The brightest and the best,
But leave me lone my journey through,
I'll set my heart at rest,
And thank God for home-sweet things, a green and friendly hill,
And red geraniums aflame upon my window sill.

Martha Haskell Clark

WHEN I READ THE TITLE of this poem, I immediately thought

of Grandma Jones. After all, she loved red geraniums and kept one on her porch in Broken Bow most summers. One of her geraniums ended up in Daddy's office for several years, where it often reminded me of her.

But then I read the poem, and I knew that this one "belonged" to Grandma Jones.

She didn't have silken gowns, jewels, or great opportunities for travel. She once told me that there was so much that she hadn't yet seen in the United States, she couldn't imagine why she would need to travel overseas. She did enjoy the few trips she was able to take, but travel wasn't something she had the opportunity to do very much of.

However, out her window on the ranch, she saw green rolling hills. In her window sills, she kept African violets. And on her porch in front of her chair were her red geraniums.

She knew how to be content with the simple things in life. Oh, she liked nice things. She was thankful for her modern conveniences, especially since she knew what it was to live without them.

I'm sure she also liked to dream. She loved to read good fiction. I have no doubt she imagined herself in other places many times during the humdrum tasks required of a ranch wife and mother.

But she had her priorities straight. She didn't need the baubles offered by the world. She kept simple beauty around her, and hers was a beautiful life. She's not remembered for jewels or silken gowns.

She is remembered instead for faithfulness, peacefulness, gentleness, kindness, humor, and love … and red geraniums.

"There's so much I haven't seen in the United States. I can't imagine why I would want to travel overseas."

~ Grandma Jones

Advice in a Twisted Tree

THE RED MAPLE TREE IN the yard is twisted. I never noticed until Bruce pointed it out the other day. Now that the leaves are all off, it is more visible. It makes me wonder what happened when it was young to make it like that. The trunk spirals around. In addition, part of the tree was broken off during an ice storm. It isn't very beautiful naked; that's all I can say about it.

However, it is my tree here at our North Carolina home. It is the tree I can see from my porch and from the bedroom window. I watch the seasons come and go on that tree. In the spring, I get to watch the leaves bud out; the tree comes alive, transformed by the power of new life. In the summer, it is beautiful. The lush green leaves offer a lovely home for the colorful birds that flit in and out. In the fall, it is magnificent. It glows with orange leaves that drift a few at a time to the ground. It is my favorite time of the year. In the late fall and winter, it's bare. It reminds me of Drayton Hall down by Charleston, South Carolina, an historic plantation house left empty on purpose so you can see the architecture. That's how the tree is. Empty. And now I can see the architecture.

I guess the twisting must have happened early on, so many years ago that no one alive knows why. Maybe it was born that way, with the twisting potential innate. On top of that, the weathering of ice storms has destroyed nearly half of the tree so that now it is a remnant of the huge tree my husband and his brothers used to climb in. But for me, it is how it's always been.

This tree kind of reminds me of Grandma McKnight. Her last twenty years were years of pain caused by a host of medical problems. Most of those illnesses were inherited. Her little body was twisted, especially her feet. They were so twisted she needed special shoes in order to walk. The neuropathy in her feet caused excruciating pain, and the medications she needed to endure it clouded her mind at times. Hers was a twisted remnant of the body she had when she was young. But even so, she shone. She prayed. She laughed. She loved. She gave advice. She lived.

When my mother died, Grandma's physician had just advised her to walk two miles a day to help her feet. The morning after they arrived at our house for Mommy's funeral, Grandma said she needed to take her walk. She wanted me to go with her, so I went. I was ten.

As we walked, Grandma explained why she was walking. "It is important to take care of your body, Miriam," she said. "That's why I'm walking." Also as we walked, she told me stories about Mommy: stories about her childhood, what kind of a child she was, things she said and did. I have never forgotten those two miles.

This morning—as I have many mornings lately—I woke up with lower back pain. There are several potential reasons, but our family history makes me think this is going to become part of my life. As I lay in bed looking out the window, I thought of Grandma and came to a decision. Today and each day, I need to walk two miles. After all, I have advice given by Grandma and a tree staring me in the face every time I sit on the porch. It would be silly not to pay attention, wouldn't it? Funny, the person who taught me how to see object lessons in nature was Grandma McKnight. But that's another story.

> *What? know ye not that your body is the temple of the Holy Ghost which is in you, which ye have of God, and ye are not your own? (1 Corinthians 6:19).*

> *"It is important to take care of your body, Miriam. That's why I'm walking."*
>
> ~ Grandma McKnight

A Legacy of Motivation

I JUST GOT BACK FROM a walk a few minutes ago. I didn't want to go. It is brisk out there. That means it feels like a windy, blustery October day in South Dakota. The thing is, I'm in South Carolina; we aren't used to that much breeziness here. Besides, I was feeling rather lazy today, the first Saturday I've been home in quite a while.

But despite all that, I did take a walk. I had decided not to; instead, I was going to write a blog post that was on my mind. But then the piece I was going to write convicted me. I hate when that happens.

Last night after I wrote about my grandparents praying for me, my husband wandered out to the kitchen. He hadn't read the blog yet, so I told him about it. He picked up an old postcard that was on the counter and looked at it. Then he said, disbelief in his voice, "This card was written to a three-year-old Miriam from Grandma McKnight. It reminds you to pray for them."

I looked up and smiled, then blubbered. Moments like that one are so awesome. I found the card in my bin of memorabilia a few weeks ago. You know the bin or box. I'm sure you've got at least one at your house too. It has my baby book, yearbooks, first report cards, craft projects my mother liked and kept, and a few pictures. I also found the post card. Here is a scan of the back.

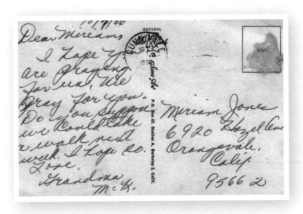

Grandma sent postcards from all over the world. Grandpa McKnight sent some too. In later years, when they weren't able to travel anymore, they wrote letters. There was always some little encouragement to live for Jesus, as well as a lot of love.

Later in the evening, I looked at the card myself. This time, it was the end of the message that got me. I cried again. Evidently, the walk I remember with Grandma after Mommy died wasn't the first one we'd taken. It wasn't the last either. And that's what got me out walking again today. Grandma taught me spiritual things as well as those that help me to be healthy. So I took a walk. Now I think I'll go pray awhile.

"The Main Thing . . ."

WHEN GRANDMA JONES WAS ABOUT 94, she shared an important concept with me. It has become one of my favorite "Grandma Jones quotes." We were talking about weight loss, and she told me this: "The main thing with your weight, Miriam, is to keep the first number a one." I laughed, but she was dead serious. In fact, even in the nursing home, she bemoaned the fact that with the "rich foods" she was served, she was having trouble keeping the first number a one.

I believed Grandma. She is my model for weight loss, after all. You see, she struggled her entire adult life with her weight. Once she started having babies, she got heavier and heavier. Sometime right around her sixtieth birthday, she determined to lose weight. I never asked her what inspired her, but it wouldn't surprise me if it was the big 6-0. All I know is that she joined a TOPS (Take Off Pounds Sensibly) Club and lost a lot of weight. In fact, she lost so much that she was the TOPS queen for her area that year. That was a huge accomplishment.

I would venture a guess that besides her marriage, children, and grandchildren, the weight loss was her proudest accomplishment. She kept her crown in the china cabinet on top of the dishes. Over the years, she gained part of the weight back, but she had that line she wouldn't cross. She was determined to keep the first number a one.

I too have struggled through the years. I'm an expert of sorts at dieting, since I read another book on the subject every time I start a new diet. It helps  motivate me. I've experienced some success, and the first number is still a one. But, I am stuck, and I know that it is not good for my health. I just can't seem to get it off and keep it off.

I have been looking at old pictures, and I find it striking to see the change in Grandma. I was putting together a power-point presentation, and Mom sent a picture of my first nursing school graduation in 1984. I realized with one glance that I had found my goal. That is what I want to look like. I checked online, and what I weighed then is right smack in the middle of where I should be.

So, I think I'll try again. I have my inspiration. I have that line I will not cross, I have my goal. But, most of all, I have the example from Grandma Jones that it is never too late to make a big change in your life. In fact, it might end up being one of your proudest moments.

"The main thing with your weight, Miriam, is to keep the first number a one!"

~ Grandma Jones

Legacy in a Little Black Book

I WAS PACKING THINGS TO move one day when I was distracted by a memory, an unexpected reminder of a legacy.

Let me explain. I've developed a reputation of sorts for being a keeper of the history. I'm not that great at organization, but through my books, blogs, our family cookbook, and the family newsletter, I've been labeled. A few years ago, my dad's cousin offered me a little notebook. It's the kind of thing that most people would throw away. It's one of those 3×4 inch, black six-ring binders that people used to keep in their purses for recording things. Some of us still keep little notebooks on hand.

At the time, I remember looking at the book and wondering why I should take it. I was intrigued by the intricate record keeping, but what on earth would I ever do with it? However, because of who it belonged to, I waffled. Besides, I didn't want to hurt my cousin's feelings, so I accepted it. I figured it would go home with me, be put "away" somewhere, and be moved from place to place until someday my nieces and nephews would throw it out.

This notebook belonged to Aunt Beulah, Grandpa Jones' youngest sister. Beulah Jones never married and never had children of her own. She had character. She was a character. But most of all, she loved her family and her God.

Every time I graduated, I could always depend on a card and a little money from Aunt Beulah. She remembered her nieces and nephews. She remembered their children. There are a lot of us. It wasn't an easy task.

When I became an aunt, I patterned my aunthood after Aunt Beulah. I remembered birthdays. When I heard about the trips she took several of her nieces and nephews on, I decided I would do that too. That's where the "eight-year-old trip" that my sister and I take with our nieces and nephews originated. I loved on them and tried to help instill good life lessons and Bible values. I wanted to be the Beulah Jones of my generation.

As I packed, Aunt Beulah was about the farthest thing from my mind. But there it was, the black notebook. I realized what it was and thought of throwing it away right then and there. Instead, I sat down to take a closer look. Shouldn't I do at least that much before discarding it?

In this notebook, she recorded every cash receipt and cash payment—down to the penny—from 1954-1964. She wrote in tiny, exact lettering. Every time I look at it, I am amazed and a little chagrined. My little notebooks are scribbled messes, and there certainly is no order to them. Besides, every attempt to write down what I've spent ends in failure.

As I leafed through, it occurred to me that the year I was born was included in this time period. Do you suppose? Nah! That would be incredible!

Fingers fumbling, I turned to May 1962 and found my birth date. Peering over my glasses—the page right up to my eyes to better focus on the tiny print—I scanned the page and caught my breath. There I was, under Cash Payments, on May 21st. "Gifts for

Cheryl and Miriam $4.03."

I wanted to laugh and cry at the same time. She has been gone a lot of years, but she is still giving me gifts.

She was caring. She was thoughtful. She was predictable. Three things I want to be. I think I still want to be the Aunt Beulah of my generation—just without the little black book. I wonder what my nieces and nephews will find when they go through my stuff some day. I hope they find caring, thoughtful, and predictable! Mostly, I hope they find love.

He Loved Her

Beareth all things, believeth all things, hopeth all things, endureth all things.

~ 1 Corinthians 13:7–8

I MADE APPLE CRISP TODAY. I also made pear crisp. It's a baking sort of day here. It's raining and cooler, although that is all relative. It is still in the 70s, but that's down from the 90s, so it feels like baking weather.

I have coffee at my side, music playing on the stereo, and I'm thinking of Grandpa McKnight. He would have been sitting right here, waiting not so patiently for the pear crisp to come out of the oven. He might have preferred peach, but he sure would have enjoyed the pear crisp. When it was out of the oven and cooled, he would say something like, "Susie, on your way back from the kitchen, you could bring me a dish of that pear crisp." Never mind that I wasn't even on my way to the kitchen, let alone on my way back.

I can't eat a pear or a peach without thinking of Grandpa McKnight. Part of it is that the last thing I saw him eat was a pear. Add to that the memory of him asking me for some peach cobbler at dinner the day he died and, well, you see how it is.

Another reason has to do with the care he provided for Grandma. She was an invalid for the last twenty years of her life. His entire schedule revolved around making sure she got her medications at the correct time, making sure she made it to her doctor's appointments, making sure she got the best care possible. He even made sure she enjoyed legal sweets.

What? Yep. They were both known to have a serious sweet tooth. For example, I know for a fact that Grandpa stashed Hostess cupcakes in the car where Grandma couldn't get to them. I also know for a fact that someone sneaked goodies in for Grandma because I caught her fishing them out from under her bed one day.

You see, she had a problem with sugar. She was borderline diabetic, and whenever she ate sugar, the neuropathy in her feet worsened. What was already excruciating became unbearable. So Grandpa developed his baking ability.

He loved fruit desserts—she loved sweets of any kind—so he made pies. He perfected the art of making fruit pies with artificial sweeteners, and they were both satisfied. So, any time I make a fruit dessert, I think of him. I think of the love and dedication that kept him at Grandma's side. I remember the lost sleep because she needed pills at midnight and again at six a.m. I remember the admiration in his voice when he spoke of Grandma's many talents. I remember that he loved her.

The Girl on the Staircase

HAVE YOU EVER BEEN AN unwitting eavesdropper? You know what I mean. You find yourself trapped somewhere you can't leave, yet you are hearing a conversation you aren't a part of.

I remember one such conversation that was a pivotal moment in my life. It happened the morning of my mother's funeral.

I was on my way down the stairs from my bedroom when I heard voices in the hallway below. I slowed as I realized that it was Daddy and Grandpa McKnight, and I could tell they were having a serious conversation. I'm not the most sensitive about not interrupting, as anyone who knows me can tell you, but, the fact that everything was skewed sideways in my life slowed me a bit.

I stopped on the staircase. I didn't want to interrupt. But, if I went back upstairs, they would probably hear me. So I just waited. What I heard was an incredible gift to a ten-year-old whose security had just taken a near fatal blow.

"Marvin, no matter what, you'll always be our son," my grandpa said.

Now, I'm sure Grandpa was struggling with his own feelings at that point. My mother was his oldest daughter, and by all accounts, they were truly kindred spirits. But yet, in the midst of his grief at her untimely and very sudden passing, he did something that not only gave my dad the strength he needed that day but provided a lifetime of security to the little girl on the staircase.

What an incredible gift.

"We are so thankful for the wonderful job your mom has done in raising you three children."

~ Grandpa McKnight

A Legacy of Good Intentions

For a just man falleth seven times, and riseth up again: but the wicked shall fall into mischief.

~ Proverbs 24:16

WHEN I AM DEAD AND gone and our nieces and nephews have to go through all of our stuff (we're trying to keep it whittled down, honest, kids), they are going to find my journals.

Before you get all excited and imagine the author's biographical record going to press, think again. Oh, it will be a biography of sorts. I'm afraid it will be a record of my very personal, very real struggle with consistency and self-discipline.

Let me explain.

I have dozens of journal books I've collected over the years. Some are flowery with beautiful lace and roses. Some have bright happy-flower covers. Some are plain black or brown leather. Some are simple composition books. Some have most of the pages full, but very few are completely full. Some have the first few pages written on and then nothing else.

For my organized niece, it would be a nightmare to try and make any sense out of the books because they are not chronological. A book may begin with a notation from 1995 and then three pages later a note starting with the date 2001. You see, what happens is good intentions.

I know that I do better with my time with God if I use a journal. But I struggle with consistency. I start a journal book, I go great guns and receive such awesome blessings, and then … well, I stop. I fail.

But a few days, weeks, or months later, I pick myself up and try again. The problem is I can never find the journal. Yes, I know. It's another sign of disorganization. So, I either start a new one or pick up another partially used one, put the date in it, and go forward.

Sometimes, I re-read sections of the notebooks. I did that this morning, and I received such a blessing from finding what I was thinking back in September of 2007.

I hope that when our nieces and nephews find these journals, they look past the obvious failure of consistency to the determination to get up and try again.

I hope they notice that the books that are finished are full because I used them to take notes in church. I hope it encourages them to make sure they are getting fed spiritually in a good church—one where taking notes is possible.

I hope they see that while Aunt Miriam didn't have it all together, she knew where to go to get it all together.

Section 2

A Legacy of Spiritual Sensitivity

Culture or Love of God?

For the love of Christ constraineth us;

~ 2 Corinthians 5:14

WHEN MR. JIMMY PRAYED IN church on Sunday, I got stuck on his first phrase, and I must admit I didn't hear much else he said. He started like this. "Dear Heavenly Father, thank you for the privilege of coming to you today."

Privilege. He said privilege.

I am a PK. (That means preacher's kid to those of you who don't know.) Daddy is a Baptist minister and has been most of my life. In fact, he was in seminary when I was born and is still going strong.

I love church. My week is not complete if I don't go to church Sunday morning, Sunday night, and Wednesday evening. Call me weird, but that is who I am. That's my culture.

Because of that, I feel comfortable here in the South. Out West, people are more private about their faith. They don't speak as freely about their church affiliations. When you pray in a restaurant, you stand out; you are conspicuous. Not here. Here, there is nothing unusual about a table full of people bowing their heads to pray before eating their meal at the local café.

Jesus is a big part of the culture in the South, and I love it.

However, I have to wonder sometimes if that's all it is to us. A part of our culture. That's why my mind got stuck on the word "privilege." I'm so blessed to know it is my privilege to come to God, to attend church. But do I look at it as a privilege? Am I attending church for the right reasons? I'm sure God is pleased that I am there, regardless of my motives, but am I receiving the full blessing I could? These are some questions I ask myself.

After the prayer, I pulled myself together and listened as our pastor preached on the love of God. He spoke of the truth that it is the love of God that constrains us.

Ah, there is the answer. Church attendance shouldn't be because it's my culture. It should be simply because God loves me, and that love is so powerful, so overwhelming, that I can't wait to get there.

It's like when I am going home to South Dakota to see my family. I can't wait for that plane to land or the car to travel those last hundred miles. I go every chance I get. I make sacrifices so that I can go. If I don't go often enough, I become unhappy. (My husband might even use the word crabby.) The love for my family constrains me to go. There would be something wrong if I went simply because it was my culture.

That's what bothered me when Mr. Jimmy prayed. The love of God should constrain me, not the culture to which I was born. After all, as a child of the living God, it is my privilege to be in church.

It's something to think about, isn't it?

Not Just for Men

I HAVE BEEN DOING A women's Bible study on the book of Nehemiah. I've learned that it is important to find a study technique that works for me and then use it to study the Bible, and that technique is my favorite. I remember my mother often used *Our Daily Bread* devotional. I remember seeing both of my mothers reading their Bibles, studying for Sunday school, or preparing a lesson for a group of ladies. But, serious in-depth Bible study—that's something I hadn't really thought of as a girl's pursuit. Until Grandma Onstott, that is.

Grandma Naomi was a traditional woman in many ways. She was a great cook, housekeeper, mother, and wife. She supported her husband through every step of his life until the Lord took her to heaven.

However, she had one underlying belief that made her something more than your average housewife. She believed in studying the Word of God—in depth.

When I was nineteen, she was sent home to die. She'd been—finally—diagnosed with multiple myeloma, and the doctors were unable to help. So, Mom and I, with my little sister in tow, packed up our bags and went to Rapid City to help care for Grandma.

Daddy, Cheryl, and Clark stayed in Gillette, Wyoming, two

hours away. They would come over every week or two. For several months, Mom and I took turns sleeping on the couch by Grandma's hospital bed in the living room. During church services, we took turns staying with Grandma while everyone else went to church.

At the time, I was taking some secretarial classes, but I was pretty sure that wasn't what I wanted to do with my life. It wasn't a very difficult decision to quit school to care for Grandma, and I've never regretted that decision. The lessons I learned while caring for her and then while keeping house for Grandpa after she died were so critical to me becoming who I am.

One Sunday evening I was sitting with Grandma, and she decided she felt good enough to do some studying. She pulled out her Bible and notebook and proceeded to work on her "homework." Grandpa was giving a college class at the church, and she had been taking it before she got sick. She explained that what she was doing was diagramming the book of Romans.

Diagramming the book of Romans? When she said that, I'm sure my face gave me away. It does that quite often, actually. What I was thinking was probably something like, WHY? HOW? WHY?

Grandma looked me in the eye and said something I've never forgotten. "It's not just the men who need to study the Bible."

That shut me up, for sure. Of course, looking back at her life, I can see this was a pattern. When Grandpa decided God was calling him to be a minister, it wasn't just Grandpa who went to Bible college. Oh no. They packed up the whole family, and Grandpa, Grandma, and their three oldest—all girls—enrolled at Pillsbury Baptist Bible College. I don't know how they did it financially, but they did.

After all, it's not just the boys who need to study the Bible. I think I'll stick to my Bible study books, though; I never did like diagramming.

"It's not just the men who need to study the Bible."

~ Grandma Naomi Onstott

Live For Jesus

"Live for Jesus!"

~ Grandpa McKnight

WHEN GRANDPA MCKNIGHT DIED IN 1997, he left a cassette tape with his "Final Words for the Family." We sat around my aunt's living room and listened to him work his way down, from oldest to youngest. At the end of each comment, he would say, "Live for Jesus." That was the bottom line for him. He just wanted his children and grandchildren to know that the most important thing for a successful, happy life is to live for Jesus.

If you split those three words up and take them one by one, I think it increases the impact. The first one is LIVE. Don't simply exist from day-to-day. Live! Find God's will and do it. I don't believe for a minute that those thirty-three miners in Chile who were rescued in 2010 will just slog through each day. I'm sure they are ready to LIVE.

The second word is "for." There has to be a purpose in our living. What are we living FOR? If we want to have the best life possible, we should be living FOR the last word: JESUS. This means we aren't living for our culture, our family, ourselves, our friends, but for Jesus and for Him alone.

When we live for Jesus, then our focus is right, and we will find the most awesome life possible. Jesus has a plan for each of us. He knows the best choices and the right paths.

It's simple, like Grandpa said: Live. For. Jesus.

I've mentioned before that phrases often prompt a song in my mind. The chorus I always find myself humming after thinking of Grandpa's last words comes from Evie, a Christian singer from the late 70s and 80s.

> Live for Jesus!
> That's what matters.
> And when other houses crumble, mine is strong.
> Live for Jesus!
> That's what matters.
> That you see the light in me and come along.

They Let God Use Them Like He Made Them

MY TWO MATERNAL GRANDFATHERS WERE both Baptist ministers. That, in and of itself, led to comparison. But, comparison isn't usually good, is it?

Grandpa McKnight and Grandpa Onstott were both faithful servants of God. They loved their wives, children, and grandchildren. They each had a wonderful sense of humor. But that's about where the similarities stopped.

Grandpa McKnight was born and raised in Kansas City and grew up a latchkey kid. When he was four, his father died and, by his own account, he was spoiled. His mother made every effort to bring him up well, and when she remarried, his stepdad tried to help him grow into a good man. He went to Sunday school—most of the time. Sometimes he would skip, but then his Sunday school teacher would show up on Saturday to say, "Bud, we missed you." It became easier to go than to face her visits.

He met Grandma at a "street meeting," and they fell in love. He was younger than she was, and her family didn't approve. He had to get permission from his mother to marry, and they eloped.

He became a "preacher boy" and studied under some really great men of God. He was a pastor in several states and loved working with college-age young people. He loved people, and people loved him. He was like a big teddy bear. He was a big man with a personality to match.

He couldn't get over the love and mercy that God extended to him, and it showed in his preaching and ministry. If you were to choose one trait of God to describe him, it would be the love of God.

Grandpa Onstott was born to farm people in Nebraska—one of eleven children. Times were hard, and they ate oatmeal every morning for breakfast. That's what they had, and they were thankful for it. He didn't eat oatmeal later in life because he couldn't stand it. If it was all they had, though, I'm sure he would have eaten it—like it or not.

He too fell in love and married young. They began farming and raised a family. They were disciplined people. They were hard workers who believed if a job was worth doing, it was worth doing right! They were German. Stoic.

They visited a church, and the whole family got saved. A few years later, Grandpa and Grandma left the farm and, with their college-age children, went to Bible college. Yes, Grandpa, Grandma, and all three daughters were enrolled together. My uncle, their son, was still in high school.

Grandpa was the pastor of several churches in Montana and South Dakota. The Bible truth that God was in charge, in control, holy, and righteous resonated with him personally, and He never got over it. He really liked the truth that God is sovereign, and it showed in every part of his ministry. He often came across as stern to people who didn't know him well, people who weren't aware of his silly side.

Grandpa McKnight and my mother were very close; they were of one mind. I am who I am genetically, much because he was who he was. From him, I get my quirky sense of humor, my humming happy personality. After Mommy died, being near Grandpa was a little like being with her still. His love for us and our daddy was unfailing. He even loved our new mother and did nothing to make her uncomfortable. In fact, he bent over backwards to encourage Daddy to marry her and then let her know that she was now part of the family.

Grandpa Onstott was so wise that he could see right through me. It was like he was an old-time prophet; I couldn't put anything past him. But he loved me, and he gently taught me how to live in the reality that God has a plan for my life and that I can trust it. He encouraged me to follow the opportunities God put in front of me. That year that I sat and listened to him process the loss of his wife of almost forty-five years built a bond that nothing ever destroyed.

But how could two men have such differing views on the character of God? Oh, they both preached all the attributes of God. Grandpa McKnight believed that God is sovereign, and Grandpa Onstott believed with all his heart that God is loving. But still, my mind—that likes things all wrapped up in a neat package—wondered at these "differences."

In the late 80s, I completed a women's Bible study book about the attributes of God. It helped me understand that we can't put God in one box. All of his attributes work together in such a way that none cancels out any other. God is all-loving, yet He is holy. His holy righteousness never overrides His love, and the fact that He is all-loving cannot negate his righteousness. God is sovereign, but that is aided by the fact that he is omniscient (all-knowing) and loving. No, our minds cannot completely understand these truths. That's why it is called FAITH.

For the past year or so, God has allowed me to add another level of understanding. I found a clip on YouTube by Tony Evans where he spoke about the power of being yourself, the power of realizing that God made you just the way you are so that He can use you for His glory. I immediately thought of my two maternal grandfathers, those two very different men of God.

Grandpa McKnight—that sweet, funny, great big teddy bear of a man who loved you no matter what—connected with the love of God because that fit his personality. He was being who God made him to be, and with that personality, he was serving God one hundred percent.

Likewise, Grandpa Onstott—stoic German prophetic lover of all that is holy—connected with the sovereignty of a righteous, holy God. He was being who God made him to be, and with that personality, he was serving God one hundred percent.

So, here I am today telling you *that* is my plan—to let God use me how He made me and to serve Him one hundred percent.

I will praise thee; for I am fearfully and wonderfully made: marvelous are thy works; and that my soul knoweth right well (Psalm 139:14).

A List of Names

WHEN GRANDPA AND GRANDMA MCKNIGHT died four days apart, my uncle, who was executor, wanted the grandkids to put their names on things they would like. That way, we all would get something that was particularly special to us. When we were in the kitchen, we found a bunch of papers on the table. They were lists. Lists of people's names, including ours.

"What are these?" My sister held them up.

I smiled. "Those were Grandma's lists. She told me she kept them so when she dozed off in the middle of praying, she could remember where she left off when she awoke. As soon as she prayed for someone, she wrote their name down. She didn't want to miss any of us."

Grandma suffered a tremendous amount of pain for many years, and her medications made her doze off. Yet because of the intense pain, she couldn't stay asleep. Most nights she was up a good share of the time, and she would spend it praying for her family and friends. She was a prayer warrior.

Grandpa was an early bird. I remember as a child waking up to find him already gone and over in his office at the church. He would get up at five or six, and mornings were his prayer and study time. When he was managing Grandma's pain meds those last few years, he had to be up until midnight to give her a dose, and then he would be back up at six. When he died, he had been spending his mornings writing a Greek lexicon. But he also prayed. For us. He was a prayer warrior.

Grandpa and Grandma Onstott had family devotions each morning. They usually read a page from the classic daily devotional, Spurgeon's Morning and Evening, a chapter from the Bible, and then they would pray. They would pray for their siblings, their children, their grandchildren, and their friends. They would pray for the nation, for the president, for all leaders. I admit that many mornings the devotions seemed long, but I would give anything to be able to sit at the table again and hear Grandpa Onstott pray in that low, rumbling, rich voice. They were prayer warriors.

My parents have a list they pray through in their family devotions. In addition, ever since they got married thirty-nine years ago, they have prayed together each night before bed. I lived at home a lot longer than most, so I know that sometimes they pray in the living room if one of them has to go to bed early. I've heard them pray. They pray for me. They are prayer warriors.

When three of our grandparents died within six weeks in 1997 and 1998, it really hit me hard. These were the people who loved me no matter what. These were the rock we all turned to when Mommy died. These were the grandparents who accepted our new Mom into the family with open arms. And likewise, the Onstotts accepted us. They prayed for us.

Who was going to take their place? I know my parents pray for me each day. I have a friend in Wyoming who has prayed for me regularly since 1989, and another friend or two have me on their prayer list ... but what about all of those other people my grandparents prayed for? Who will pray for them? Will I notice a difference? Will they?

I know that God is able to come up with other prayer warriors, and for that, I'm really and truly thankful. Personally though, I am still challenged in my prayer life. I need to be praying more. I need to be to another generation what my grandparents and parents were to me. A legacy of prayer must not be wasted.

Always in every prayer of mine for you all making request with joy (Philippians 1:4).

Treasure in a Bible

WHEN WE WERE AT MY parents' in December, I found a real treasure. I was in the basement and saw an old Bible sitting on top of the piano. I picked it up and opened it. It was Mommy's Bible. I stood there, unmoving, while I leafed through it. I found the underlined places—she loved some of the same passages I do—and notes she had written in the margin.

I love Philippians. I especially like Philippians 4. I actually have a very strong memory of my mother using Philippians 4:8 to correct bad thoughts I was having as a child. It stuck with me.

So, there in Daddy's basement, I looked for the red highlights, the underlined places, the torn pages, and the notes in the margins. These are the verses that jumped out at me.

Philippians 4:4–8

> Rejoice in the Lord always: and again I say, Rejoice.

> Let your moderation ("sweet reasonableness" is written in the margin) be known unto all men. The Lord is at hand.

> Be careful for (anxious about) nothing: but in every thing by prayer and supplication with thanksgiving let your requests be made known unto God.

And the peace of God which passeth all understanding shall keep your hearts and minds through Christ Jesus.

Finally, brethren, whatsoever things are true, whatsoever things are honest, whatsoever things are just, whatsoever things are pure, whatsoever things are lovely, whatsoever things are of good report: if there be any virtue, and if there be any praise, think on these things.

I love that the Bible is the same now as it was when she was a young mother. I love that God can speak to me in the same way.

After several minutes, I came to the back fly leaf, and that's where I found the real treasure. There, tucked inside the back cover, was a little card. You could see it had been taped on that page, but the tape had long ago come loose, and now it was just tucked in place. The card is faded. There are yellowed tape spots at the top and bottom. But it is one of the most beautiful pieces of paper I have ever seen.

MY PLEDGE TO PRAY

This is to remind me that on *Nov. 19, 1962*
I promised to pray "that the God of our Lord Jesus Christ, the Father of glory, may give unto _____ *Cheryl and Miriam Jones* the Spirit of wisdom and revelation in the knowledge of Christ"* and His will for life and Christian service.
*Eph. 1:17

Signed *Dean Ann Jones*
                    mother

CONSERVATIVE BAPTIST MISSION SOCIETIES
Wheaton, Illinois

The fact that my mother not only gave me life but desired to do anything she could to ensure that I would have "the Spirit of wisdom and revelation in the knowledge of Christ and His will for (my)  life" overwhelms me. I am so blessed.

I believe that on November 19, 1962, the Sovereign God wasn't just working in a mother's heart so that she would pray for her little girls. I believe God was preparing a card so that forty-eight years later, that little six-month-old girl could experience some Mommy-love. Thank you, Jesus.

A Dome of Protection

BECAUSE IT WAS SUCH A mild winter, there seem to be a lot of mosquitoes and bugs out this summer. Last year a local child died from a mosquito bite. So, I decided I didn't want to be eaten up, and I sure didn't want to die at the hand—or sucker—of a mosquito.

At the store, we found these nifty little contraptions that you turn on, and a little fan blows repellant all around you. I was quite skeptical that it would work but was willing to give it a try. I have to say it seems to have worked. Every time I go to the garden, I put it on. I haven't been bitten once since I started using it—and Bruce calls me "skeeter bait" because of how they're attracted to me much more than to him. I'm impressed.

This weekend on TV, we saw a commercial for this product. It showed a lady on her knees weeding, and around her was this dome. All of the mosquitoes came diving in to attack her and crashed into the dome. She simply looked over her shoulder and smiled. I laughed.

This morning the Lord brought that commercial to mind when I was thinking about my nieces and nephews and my sincere desire to be the person who prays God's protection around them. In my mind, I imagined my prayers going up to God. I imagined the dome of protection descending around them, and I saw Satan's darts bouncing off.

That is my goal. That is my promise to my nieces and nephews. Your Aunt Miriam will be praying for you. She will be storming God's gates asking the one with ALL POWER to cover you with a dome of protection.

If you step out of God's protection, I will be praying that God tugs you back in. I will always love you. I will always pray for you, for so long as I live.

That is my promise to you.

Section 3

A Legacy of Family

My Husband Took Me Skype Hunting!

GRANDMA WASN'T A FRIVOLOUS PERSON. She was frugal. However, she was quite able to enjoy a modern convenience or ten! As a young wife and mother, she lived in a one-room sod house with no power, no phone, and no heat source other than a wood stove in which they burned "cow chips" (pieces of dried manure). So, later in life when she had the ability and means, she did enjoy the basic modern conveniences we enjoy today. If her TV broke down, she was quick to call a repairman. If he couldn't fix it, she arranged for a moderately priced new one to be delivered. She had electricity, a telephone, radio, microwave, dishwasher, washer, dryer, refrigerator, stove, a hot water heater ... all things she didn't have the ability to enjoy when she was young. Once she could afford them and understood how these things could make her life better, she was a fan.

I like modern conveniences too. However, I am a little suspicious of a lot of the newfangled contraptions. Okay, I admit it. I don't really like learning new stuff. I get comfortable with my techno-ability level and don't like it when it's stretched. In addition, I am leery of things that seem to be "all the rage," especially when most of what I hear about them in the news is how they are used for nefarious purposes. I am never the first to try something; I usually wait until someone I know has tried it, or the new fad has become mainstream.

So, several months ago when my husband suggested a webcam for our new computer, I was resistant. Well, actually, I think my words were, "I don't think we need that." He proceeded to share some of the positive things about having one. He suggested that I could talk with family and friends who live far, far away. For instance, my sister in Thailand. I still was resistant. I really couldn't see my family jumping on the webcam bandwagon. He also suggested that he could use it in preparing for the college chemistry classes he teaches. That made sense, so I agreed.

Last week I spent a morning baking. My husband decided to download Skype® to both of our computers and see if he could get us up and running. He explained again that he was pretty sure my sister in Thailand already had a webcam in her laptop. If, he explained, we went on Skype®, we could talk and see each other at the same time. In addition, if someone back home in South Dakota got one, our parents could also talk to us. So, as geeky as it sounds, we spent an hour or so practicing with Skype®, me in the living room and my husband in his office. Visualizing the possibilities, I made the leap from skeptical to interested. Events quickly led us to purchase a webcam for my parents for Christmas and have them pick it up locally. On Christmas Eve, my sister and I were both able to visit with our parents.

I have discovered that the best presents don't always cost much. Other than the slight additional fee when we bought the computers, and our parents' webcam, this present was free. It wasn't even meant as a Christmas gift. It was simply one of those things my husband thinks of to make my life easier or more joyful. He's really good at that. Besides, he's reaping the benefits too: I was forced to admit that I really shouldn't question his ideas since they're almost always right.

I wish we could have shared this modern convenience with Grandma. She would have loved being able to see family members who lived far away. But, that wouldn't have been better than having them come see her, especially the new babies. You can't hold babies *via* Skype®.

Faith of My Father

THIS MORNING IN CHURCH, WE sang the song that is sung in many churches on Father's Day. It has become something of a Father's Day Anthem.

As often happens with routine, I tuned out the beginning. Admittedly, it might have been subconscious since the first couple of verses are so grim that my "happy-ending-loving heart" cringes at the words and descriptions. I know it is a part of the fallen world, but I only tolerate hearing about it so much, and then I'm done.

Anyway, something brought me back to the words of the song as we started the last verse. I believe it was the Holy Spirit.

Faith of our fathers, we will love
Both friend and foe in all our strife.
And preach thee, too, as love knows how
By kindly words and virtuous life.
Faith of our fathers, holy faith!
We will be true to thee till death!

~ By Frederick W. Faber

As we sang those words, a face popped into my head. It was Daddy's face. This verse could have been written about him. This is one of the many reasons I believe I am so very blessed. You see, I have been given a father who loves both the foe and friend, preaches in love, speaks kindness, and lives a virtuous life. What a gift.

I will be true to the faith of my father.

Teachable Moments from Daddy

WHEN I WAS GROWING UP, my dad used a low-key approach to teaching life lessons, teaching the important things in life moments. Instead of reading us the list of rules, he waited for a "teachable moment" and then taught the biblical principle.

For instance, I do not remember any one conversation on swearing. He didn't give us a list of words not to say and quiz us later. He didn't even freak out if we said one. Instead, if someone around us used one of those words, he would calmly point out what the word meant, why we should never say it, or why it should only be said in its appropriate context. Therefore, without ever having the "Words Not to Say Lecture," I learned the truth of the lesson.

I still categorize words based on this approach. First, there are the obvious words that you should never say. They are rude, crude, and socially unacceptable. Usually, these words have to do with bodily functions.

Secondly, there is the category of inappropriately used words that has two sub-categories. The first is "Good Words Used Wrongly." This includes the names for God. I had no trouble understanding the problem here; after all, it is one of the Ten Commandments: "Thou shalt not take the name of the Lord, thy God in vain." I cannot say "Oh God," unless I really mean "Oh God!" I cannot say "Jesus Christ" in frustration; he died to pay my sin debt. Why would I use his name lightly or disrespectfully? A side category of these are euphemisms. As Daddy explained it, these are words that people say instead of names for God (or other words they want to say but know they shouldn't use that way). Examples are gosh, gee, golly, heck, and darn.

"God isn't fooled by us trying to white wash what we say." He even looked them up in the dictionary for us once. (gee interj [euphemism for Jesus] – used to express surprise or enthusiasm. *Webster's New Student's Dictionary*.)

Then there were other words. I like to call them the "Not-So-Good Words, Used Wrongly." There were two in particular that he explained this way. "Before you say them, make sure you know what they mean. When you say, 'God damn it,' you better think about what you are saying. Do you really want God to damn that thing or person? Do you understand what it means for God to damn something? Do you really want him to send that thing or person to hell?" This led to the second word in this particular teaching moment: hell. Why can't you use that word in moments of frustration or shock?

"Hell is a place. It is real. And it is terrible. Hell is the reason Jesus came as a baby (Christmas!) and lived among us, died on the cross, and then rose again. (Easter.) Hell is not something to trivialize."

I never heard him use these words inappropriately either, I guess that's what makes a real teachable moment. When the teacher lives what he says, it's easy to believe.

So, when the topic of the month for my writers' group was announced as "What the hell is that?" my initial response was, "Well, I guess I won't be writing to that topic!" Then someone reminded me that hell isn't primarily a swear word; it's a destination. In light of how I have learned to deal with these words, I am choosing to use it appropriately. With words straight from the Bible, I have written a poem, answering the question, "What the hell is that?"

WHAT!?! the HELL IS THAT?

It's a sorrowful pit, no eye can see,
Dark painful lonely, never set free.
A profoundly deep and empty space,
An unquenchable furious fire filled place.

A wide and welcoming gate it has,
The road to hell many shall pass.
But in its depth there's only grief,
Just weeping, wailing, gnashing of teeth.

The fallen angels, are kept in their chains,
A bottomless pit, full of infinite pains.
The smoke coming out is a horrible sight,
Ascending forever to terrible height.

The devil someday will be taken as well,
And cast into the lake of fire with hell.
A place for those who die in their sin,
Whose names in the book of life have not been.

It's eternal, everlasting, it never will end,
This place that a just God all sinners must send.
Eternal separation from an all-loving Lord,
A never ending, agonizing, sorrowful reward.

BUT it need not be a place that we go,
For God in His mercy the world did love so.
He sent His own Son to pay for our sin,
So we can eternity instead spend with Him.

With His resurrection the Lord did destroy
The power of death, and hell, oh what joy.
And if we repent, and trust in His grace
He'll give us a home in a much better place.

"God isn't fooled by us trying to whitewash what we say."

~ Daddy

A Life in Word and Deed

And whatsoever ye do in word or deed, do all in the name of the Lord
Jesus, giving thanks to God and the Father by him.

~ Colossians 3:17

I'VE HEARD THAT A GIRL gets her view of God from her father.
For some of us, that's not a good thing. For those like me, it turns
out to be a wonderful gift. My daddy has been the most influential
person in my life. Without his love, I wouldn't fully understand
the love of God. Without the discipline he meted out, I wouldn't
know the security of limits or understand the importance of a disciplined life. Almost everything he taught me fits into one of three
categories.

CHOOSE WISELY

The first thing he taught me was decision making. To live a
successful life, we must determine right from wrong, the best from
the not-so-good. By example, he taught me a simple rule of thumb.
Every decision in life should be made based on the absolute principles found in God's Word, the Bible. That may sound simplistic,
but it isn't. Or maybe it is.

"Do unto others as you would have them do to you" covers

a lot of decisions about how to act toward others. "Be ye kind one to another, tenderhearted, forgiving one another"—that gives the skinny on what to do if someone hurts you. "Know ye not that your body is the temple of the Holy Ghost?" This covers all of the bad things we can do to our bodies.

What about money decisions? It's there. There are principles for marriage, for work ethics, for raising children, dealing with employees and employers, friends, enemies—it's all there.

Over and over, Daddy would point out what was wrong with a situation, why—using the Bible principle—and what would be a better approach. He didn't focus on a list of do's and don'ts, just Bible principles.

Oh sure, there are definite do's and don'ts in the Bible, but often there are gray areas, things that aren't so clearly spelled out. Daddy's rule for that was simple. "If in doubt, don't. With the Holy Spirit living in you, doubting is a pretty good sign that it isn't such a great thing."

"Do unto Others . . ."

The second category of truths learned from my dad's life is how to treat other people. He knows what he believes, why he believes it, and he does his best to live it. This gives him a consistent walk that is demonstrated through the fruit of the Spirit. If you think about it, most of those qualities have something to do with how we relate to God and how we treat other people.

Daddy is a friend and encourager. He loves to help people who need a hand up. He believes that we should see the potential in everyone and let God tell them if they are in the wrong spot.

He is also forgiving. I've watched him deal with people who

hurt him. It is amazing to see. He just lets it go. He chooses to treat them with respect. He rarely, if ever, says something negative about someone. If he does, it's worth paying attention to and is given as a warning rather than a condemnation.

Through his daily example, I have learned how to love the unlovable, how to be patient with others and myself, the meaning of true gentleness, the difference between meekness and weakness, and self-control. The overriding Bible principle for his relationship with others is "Do unto others as you would have them do unto you." The actual verse says, "As ye would that men should do to you, do ye also to them, likewise." That's one principle my dad bases his life on. It's a powerful one.

Serve God

Besides learning how to make decisions and how to treat others, Daddy taught me how to serve God. He served as the pastor of several small churches. He started three churches and has ministered to people in four different states. Many preacher's kids have less than positive things to say about growing up in a pastor's home. They say their dad was too strict, there was never any money, the ministry took him away from his family, and they were always being watched. Not me.

It was a joy to grow up in a pastor's house. Daddy loved the ministry. He still does. He enjoyed working with people and learned to deal with the difficult ones. One day when I came home from work and complained about a patient's difficult family member, he said, "Miriam, as long as you are working with people, there are always going to be a few strange ones in your life. Don't let them ruin it for you." He chose to love people but kept his focus on God and the task God had for him.

He made being a pastor look like fun. Serving God was an adventure, a privilege, even. We were the blessed ones. He didn't complain about the long hours, the financial difficulty, the uncertainty of the future, or the pitiful retirement benefits. He knew that he was where God wanted him, and that was all he needed to know. God would provide even if it meant Daddy worked a second job.

He empowered us to believe that we could be anything God wanted us to be. There are no limits when you are in the will of God. There is no greater satisfaction in life than to be what God wants you to be. The greatest joy comes from serving.

I learned what it means to have a servant's heart. When I was a teenager, one of our chores was helping to clean the church each week. He explained the principle—if you are faithful in this menial job, then God will bless you with a less menial job. Years later, when it was my week to clean the church, Daddy was at the church, studying. "Why am I still cleaning the church?" I asked, tongue-in-cheek. He looked at me, gave me that sly grin and said, "I didn't say you wouldn't still have to clean the church; I said He would give you other jobs too. He has, hasn't he?" Humph! He had me there. Daddy has never been above doing whatever needs done, even if it's cleaning toilets.

Another thing he taught me was how to plug along, even when you don't see the results. A pastor has a tough job. There may be months, even years when the growth in the church is slow, stops, even goes backwards. Often, progress is measured more in the lives that are changed, the growth in the hearts of people, rather than in the numbers of people attending. From this I learned that quality is definitely more important than quantity. The bottom line is this: if you are in the will of God, then all you are responsible to do is to be faithful. God will take care of the results. This may be the most valuable lesson I ever learned from my dad: humble faithfulness.

Wow, you may say. Your dad must have spent a lot of time explaining and talking to you. I know he spent time explaining these things to us, but the truth is that most of the lessons I learned from him I learned by watching. You see, the lessons he taught most effectively were the ones he lived. When someone consistently demonstrates the truth, it's a powerful thing, much more powerful than words.

A Gift Beyond Measure

My mother's favorite verses

It is of the LORD's mercies that we are not consumed, because his compassions fail not. They are new every morning; great is thy faithfulness.
~ Lamentations 3:22–23

JANUARY 11TH IS THE ANNIVERSARY of the day my world changed forever. On January 11, 1973, my mother got up from the couch to go fix supper, and in the doorway between the dining room and kitchen, she went to heaven instead.

It was sudden. It was unexpected. It was final.

There is no way that such an event doesn't affect a child. I know there are several parts of my character that were affected by this life event. Thankfully, a great daddy and extended family helped keep a lot of the potential problems at bay. Eventually, a new mom helped set my world right. But still . . .

I was talking to Aunt Rachel this morning, and we were remembering that day. She shared some of her memories with me from that time, and we spoke of Mommy. I told her that my biggest regret is that I didn't get to know her as an adult. I have dreamed of having one afternoon with her, just to know what she was like. Her three sisters, her parents, my daddy, and even my stepmom have shared what they could, and my oldest McKnight aunt did some more of that today.

"She was a lot like Mother," she said.

I could see that. I know that, like Grandma, my mother demonstrated an unusual ability to see the spiritual application in almost any situation. She loved God. She loved her husband and her children. She loved her parents and sisters. She loved people, and people loved her.

She was exceptionally gifted. It seemed that everything she tried, she did well. She was a talented musician: a fine pianist with a beautiful voice. She was a gifted speaker. She was an amazing typist and secretary. She was a wonderful manager. She was an awesome wife and mother. She was a beloved pastor's wife. She wrote great letters.

When my parents left college and moved to San Francisco for seminary, they were moving far from family. Back then, phone calls were expensive, so they were few and far between. Every week she typed a letter using carbon paper and would send the letter to her parents and the carbon copy to her sister at college. As the years went by, she continued the practice, adding copies for her two other sisters.

Aunt Rachel kept all of her copies. She missed my mother, and the letters made her feel closer. When Mommy died, she possessed a treasure trove. In 1992, she sent each of us the treasure. She made three copies of all of those letters—thirteen years' worth—and put them into institutional notebooks for us. Two notebooks each. There were a lot of letters.

I spent that summer reading them. I personally love reading journals and books of letters. It's really the best way to learn history.

This was my history. Mommy had a way of writing about everyday events that brought my childhood to life for me. In addition, it was from her perspective, and I found myself becoming friends in my heart with this woman. As I neared the end, I didn't want to finish. I knew how it ended, and I didn't like it.

The last entry was a card Mommy had sent to Rachel. The verse on the card said this:

> We can't buy peace, **Or an extra day**
> A single star, Or the sun's warm ray.
> We can't buy trust; We can't buy love;
> All of these are gifts from God above.
>
> --Helen C. Butler

It was written December 28, 1972.

I pulled the book out again today and read a bit. Such a gift, a gift beyond measure.

An Open Letter to My Mom

I DON'T KNOW IF YOU realize what a precious gift you were to us, to me. When you came to our home, we were a fractured family: heads down, just doing the next thing that needed done while coping the best we could with the tsunami caused by Mommy's death. Oh, we had love. We had family support. We had friends. We had an awesome daddy.

But the hole was immense and deep, an endless chasm.

And then you came.

The relief was immediate and exhilarating. Well, at least until you fixed creamed tuna and spinach. <Smile.> You came with your new foods, your new ways, and your breath of fresh air.

You were really cool because you were a single missionary. You were the most amazing woman in the world because you got my mass of thick, unmanageable hair cut into a shag!

91

We came home from school one day to find you and Daddy had redone our bedrooms with new comforters and paint. Oo-la-la!

Of course, you were firm. You were the mom, and that was an interesting adjustment for three children who had been motherless for long enough to have developed some independent ways. That's all I'm going to say about that.

I have a strong memory of the first time I remember an adult apologizing to me. That was you. It wasn't anything big. It was just something you said in front of others. Something I'm positive, looking back, that I would have said in the same situation. But, when you apologized to me, it did something inside of me. It made me feel like you were someone I could trust. Someone who would do right, no matter what. I learned that while saying you are sorry is VERY hard, it is the right thing. That, very possibly, is the most important lesson you ever taught me.

During all my years of being single, you were my map. You were the one who reminded me that God has a plan. I simply needed to wait. I'm thankful I had that example. It helped more than you know.

Of all of the things you did or were, the best was that you loved our daddy. You made him so happy, and that righted our world in ways I can't even describe. You continued the pattern we had seen in our parents—that of servant leadership. It's a lesson that has become part of who I am, who my siblings are.

I thought I understood how it must have been for you to come as an independent, single missionary lady and suddenly become a pastor's wife and a mother. Then I got married at forty-three and moved from South Dakota to South Florida, leaving family, friends, church, job, and everything I knew. I totally underestimated the emotional impact all of those changes would make. I was so ecstatically happy to finally be married, but I was such an emotional mess.

I couldn't help but realize just what a massive life-shattering change getting married must have been for you. Once again, you were my example.

While our life was righting itself, yours was tipped upside down. Yet, through it all, you kept an even keel. You trusted the One who is trustworthy. You made a difference. Somewhere in there, you went from being my mom to being my friend. What an awesome God we serve.

I love you, Mom. Thank you for choosing to love us.

This Day in My History

The LORD will perfect that which concerneth me:

~ Psalms 138:8

GRANDPA AND GRANDMA MCKNIGHT'S ANNIVERSARY is an important day in my history. They were married in 1937. They eloped with the permission of Grandpa's mother. Evidently, Grandma's people didn't see the qualities she valued in Grandpa. In their defense, he was younger and a latchkey kid. I know they just wanted the best for their daughter.

I am glad they got married, for obvious reasons. In addition, I am thankful for the example of their almost-sixty-one-year marriage.

Grandpa called Grandma "Lady." It was sweet and so much in character for him. It always reminded me of the song written by Lionel Richie and sung by Kenny Rogers.

Lady, I'm your knight in shining armor, and I love you.
You have made me what I am, and I am yours.

These first two lines remind me of a story Grandma told me. She said that one of the ladies from her church told her that "he wasn't much of a catch, but maybe he's a diamond in the rough." There was fire in Grandma's eyes when she told me this almost sixty years after the fact. Her look also said, "Guess she was wrong!"

I know that Grandpa believed that Grandma did polish him. He polished her too. Their marriage was not perfect. After all, like the rest of us, they had their moments. Their marriage did stand the test of time, though. When they died, four days apart, they were in love and still serving God, even from the confines of the house. What more can you ask?

Several years after they were married, a baby boy decided he had read everything on the walls of his mommy's womb, and it was time to make an appearance. After all, he liked to "learn new stuff," and he was anxious to get out in the real world and get started. So, two months early—on my grandparents' anniversary—my husband was born.

I like the connection. I like knowing that God's plan for my life included working behind the scenes to bring someone into the world who would be such an amazing match for me. There's a song I heard on the radio shortly before we were married. It is by NewSong, and one line of it says, "When God made you, He must have been thinking about me." I think it could have been written for us.

Before we were ever married, we realized in a small way how much we brought out the best in each other. However, the past eight years have confirmed it. We are better together.

We've each seen good and bad marriages over the years, and it seems to us that this is one good predictor of their success or failure. Does the couple bring out the best in each other? Does he make her a stronger person? Does she inspire him to be a better man? Does she want to be a godlier person for his sake? It's become a litmus test for us when we are counseling or talking to someone considering marriage.

It makes me sad that Grandpa and Grandma McKnight never met my husband, but I believe they would agree with God's choice for me. I think they would agree with our litmus test too.

My Mother's Sisters

MY MOTHER HAS THREE SISTERS. Mommy was the oldest and the leader of the pack. When God decided her work on earth was done, they weren't in agreement—not the least bit! I don't blame them. I wouldn't have been either if I had been her sister. No one who was left behind was ready for that; after all, she was only thirty-four. But, no matter how much you disagree with God, it isn't a productive pastime.

Through the years, our contact has been sporadically regular due to distance. The two older aunts married men they met at college and spent the majority of their lives in Georgia and Tennessee. The youngest —some of us thought she was the coolest when we were little—settled in Portland. Since we lived in the Northern Plains, seeing them wasn't an everyday occurrence.

One of my major excitements about living in the South has been the opportunity to see my aunts more. This weekend was such an opportunity. It is always an adventure, believe me.

The main thing that always smacks me in the face and puts a

perma-grin on it is the realization that there really is a reason I'm the way I am. This silly, bright, smiling, humming body I walk around in has its counterparts.

Another reason is I get to see a bit of my mother again. Each of them brings something to the table.

Aunt Rachel is the one who gave me the gift of my mother's letters. She is the organizer, the managerial leader of the group. It's a position she took only because the real leader of the pack became unavailable—and one just can't dial 1-800-4HEAVEN. Aunt Rachel has called us, sent photos, and pulled my leg my entire life. She ALWAYS kept in touch. ALWAYS.

In Aunt Connie's face and spirit, I see the reflection of my beautiful mother. The similarities are uncanny. She is such an example of a loving, godly wife and mother; it certainly gives me an incredible pattern to follow. After her children were raised, she pursued her education. Yet another lesson—you can always learn new things and change your life.

Aunt Carolyn has a gift for business and management and, indeed, travels the world teaching people in other cultures how to run businesses to help them become self- sustaining. She has pulled herself up by her bootstraps, so to speak, and I find in her a great source of advice for dealing with people issues at work and in my writing career. She has a manner of speaking that reminds me so much of Grandpa McKnight.

I know that for my aunts, our time together is always a little bittersweet. Each of their get-togethers is missing something, someone. I'm so thankful that someday—in heaven—we can ALL get together and listen to Nora Ann McKnight Jones sing again.

The Older Generation - Up for the Challenge

I LOVE THIS PICTURE FROM the Jones Reunion. It might be my favorite. To someone who doesn't know our family, it looks like nothing but a picture of a group of sixty-to-seventy-something adults. But for those of us who know these people, there are some things that might make us look a second time.

The fifth from the left is Daddy. He is surrounded by his wife, sisters, brothers-in-law, cousins, and their spouses. Oh, and his sister-in-law. This picture started as one of those spur-of-the-moment, grab a group of chatting people, make them line up, and take their picture photo-ops. I think we started with five or six. Then we noticed more from their generation in the room and called them over. There are several pictures in the series, and each has one or two more people.

My favorite part is that they are mixed up. With the exception of two couples, they aren't standing with their spouses. I love photos that give different groupings. I like the unexpected twist. Here we have a group of people who have grown up together, and their spouses have been part of the family for ten to fifty-six years—so long they are family too. They have differences of opinion, differences of belief, differences of interests, but they are family.

Another thing I like about this picture is the sheer number of years of stable marriage represented here. These folks are all in it for the long haul. They had good examples in my grandparents and their parents, all who stayed married until death parted them. In this day where families are so transient, ours stands out. I can truly say I have been surrounded by great examples.

At a store in Broken Bow, I saw a plaque. It displays a quote attributed to Ruth Bell Graham that says, "A happy marriage is a union of two good forgivers." I'm thankful for this generation and their determination to stick it out and make their love grow instead of letting it die. I love you all! I understand why you aren't quite ready to be called "the older generation," but I'm thankful for the wisdom and strength you bring. I really think you are up for the challenge. Your parents were proud of you, and we are so grateful.

Of Mice and Men

LAST WEEKEND WE HAD THE privilege of getting together with a bunch of Bradley family members. Some of them even stayed with us. We enjoyed the visitors and their willingness to put up with our "work in progress" house.

Besides the human visitors, we also found mice. After killing a mouse by accidentally stepping on it, we put out the D-Con that, just as advertised, produced some dead mousie-relatives three days later. This in turn prompted another clean-out frenzy that I'd been putting off.

In the cleaning, we discovered papers from Bruce's parents. There were receipts from medicine they bought the year Bruce was born. Since he was sickly, there were a lot. There was paperwork from when Bruce's dad was in the Korean War. There were high school diplomas for three of the boys. There were treasures his Mom stashed away.

I am sometimes sad that I never got to meet Bruce's parents. However, through cleaning out their house, I think I've come to know them better than a lot of people. Through the things we save, the things we feel important enough to keep, we show a bit of who we are. I am thankful for the opportunity to help with the project of Mama's house. It's been a huge amount of work, but at the same time it's been a special blessing.

At the Bradley family reunion, I heard more stories and finally met the only aunt and uncle that I didn't yet know. I received a blessing from the message Bruce's Uncle Robert preached in church Sunday. I loved hearing his aunt and her grandchildren sing and enjoyed making music with some of them. I learned more about Bruce's dad from his brothers and sons. I remember looking around at the roomful of people and thinking, these are my kind of folks.

I was reminded about another Bradley get-together. The fall after we were married, we drove from Florida up to North Carolina for a visit. Bruce invited his aunts, uncles, and other extended Bradley family to gather at the Golden Corral Restaurant so they could meet me. He wasn't too sure how many would show up. He was surprised. Every single local aunt and uncle was there. As we prepared to eat, his aunt's husband, a retired minister, stood to pray. As he lifted his voice to God, my heart swelled. This man was a prayer warrior. In his voice, I heard the echo of my daddy and grandpas. This could have been a gathering of my family. I felt so incredibly at home with these people.

It is awesome enough that God gave me an amazing husband, but one who has a family that I can be instantly at home with? That's incredible!

Section 4

A Legacy of Roots

"Miriam, home is where you make it."

~ Jim Jones

Roots

I LIKE TO TELL PEOPLE that if I went to the moon and there were people there, I would like it and want to stay. I'm just that way. I have lived in nine states and at least twenty-two houses. There is something special about every place I've ever lived, even the dorm rooms. All of this moving could have left me with a lack of "roots," but it didn't.

I would say that the reason I have roots is because of three of the places I've lived. Those places would be the ranch, the parsonage, and Mama's house. From my earliest memories to the present day, one or all of those places have provided a sense of belonging that I needed.

I may not have the gift of living in the same house my whole entire life like my best friend does, but I have roots nonetheless. Like my Uncle Jim told me when I got married, "Miriam, home is where you make it."

THE RANCH

The Ranch in my first book is a real place. In the summer, we would usually go visit The Ranch for a week or two. There were a couple summers when our trip coincided with some of the cousins' visits. Those were the most fabulous summers. We rode horses, cut musk thistles, picked berries, and went to the county fair in Broken Bow, Nebraska.

When my grandparents moved into town in 1983, we all went to The Ranch for the sale. It was a sad time, but we were all glad Grandpa and Grandma would be able to enjoy living in town since life on The Ranch had been growing harder and harder for them.

Now, you may wonder why I keep capitalizing the words, *The Ranch*. There is a reason. It sets it off as an Important Place. You see, The Ranch was very important to me. I can't speak for any of cousins or siblings, but I can say it was home base for me.

When I was in kindergarten, we moved back from California and actually lived on The Ranch for a couple of months while my parents sought the Lord's will concerning where they should start a church. When we moved again, it was to North Platte, less than two hours from The Ranch. For the next eight years, we lived there, going to The Ranch several times a year. It was a short enough drive that if we needed a quick "get away place" on a Friday evening, we could drive up and come back Saturday.

When I was going into eighth grade, we spent a few more months at The Ranch when Daddy was between churches. We ended up moving to California again. We were there three years, and when we came home to visit, home was The Ranch. Wherever we went, from there on, going back to The Ranch always felt like home. It was that stable place, unchanging in the midst of change.

After Grandpa and Grandma moved to town, we were thrilled when one of the cousins bought the old place. And when Grandma went to the nursing home, and they emptied out her house, the picture of The Ranch was returned to The Ranch, where it hangs today. It belonged there because The Ranch was home. Just as it has been for as long as I can remember.

The Parsonage

The church where my dad has been the pastor for the past twenty-two years is also the church where my step-grandpa was pastor when my parents were married. In fact, that's where my dad and stepmom were married. Not only that, but my sister, brother, and I each got married in that church. You can well imagine it is a special place for us.

However, not only is the church building special to us, the parsonage is too. It is—after all—a family home of sorts. The first time I ever stepped inside that home and met my new grandparents-to-be, I thought they were rich. The cathedral wood ceiling in the living room and kitchen part of the house were so spectacular to my twelve-year-old eyes; they impressed me beyond words. And that takes a lot, I'm just saying. So, for the past thirty-nine years, this house has been a family home.

It's the place where Grandma Onstott died. It's where I kept house for Grandpa until he remarried and where my parents live. It's the only house my nieces and nephews have ever known Grandpa and Grandma to live in. For them, I guess it is their "ranch."

The terraces out back are usually a riot of marigolds in the summer and, like my Grandpa Onstott, my parents have a garden. The marigolds grow like weeds, and the deer that like to think they own the yard will leave them alone, so they are a great choice. The vegetable garden, though, requires a very high fence. It is a lovely house and a lovely yard. And it is home to me.

Someday it won't be. That will be hard, I'm sure. But, when someone else lives there, the memories we've made in that house will still be safely tucked away in my head. For those, those, no one can take away.

MAMA'S HOUSE

About the time we were married, Bruce inherited his parents' house. The spring after our wedding, we drove the thirteen hours from South Florida to North Carolina to take a look. The house had been mostly uninhabited for several years. However, most of his mother's things were still there. His sister-in-law had done quite a bit of work, but the project was still impressive. We could smell mildew, so we bought two dehumidifiers, hooked them up, and headed south again.

Over the past seven years, we have worked our way north, and project by project, we have worked at cleaning out and resurrecting the home place. This place has an incredible pull, not only for Bruce, but for me.

This is the house his parents built shortly after they were married. His daddy would come home on leave from the military for a weekend to work on it before going to Korea. When Bruce and his brothers were born, this was the house to which they were carried home. When Bruce was in high school, the one small bedroom was no longer enough for four growing boys, so his dad added on another small bedroom. With that bedroom, the house was almost 800 square feet.

Now, in the past few years, we've added on an addition so it's big enough for the two of us. (I know; the math doesn't add up, does it? I guess it could be all those boxes of books and musical instruments we have.)

From the start, I felt at home here. There was never any question in my mind about this place. It was Bruce's home. It was mine. The closest I ever had to the roots we have here was the ranch and the parsonage. It is comforting for me to know that my husband has a place that has always been home. And now, they are my roots too.

I love knowing that we are maintaining and trying to improve a place his parents loved and worked so hard to keep. When I sit at the kitchen table and work on my computer, I think of his mother. She used to sit at this very table—in the old kitchen—and read and watch the birds out the window. Now, I sit at the same table in the new kitchen—right in the spot where the tree she watched used to stand—and watch the birds out on the deck.

Bruce's Aunt Alva tells us his mama would have loved what we've done. That is music to my ears. Beautiful music.

Going Home / Beautiful Nebraska

Nebraska State Song Lyrics:

Beautiful Nebraska

Written by Jim Fras

Chorus:
Beautiful Nebraska, as
you look around,
You will find a rain-
bow reaching to the
ground.
All these wonders by
the Master's hand,
Beautiful
Nebraskaland.

We are so proud of
this state where we
live.
There is no place that has so much to give.

AS A CHILD LIVING IN Nebraska, I learned the state song. How
or where I learned it, I don't really know. I assumed I learned it

at school, but my older sister believes that we learned it when our mother sang it for a Historical Society event. At any rate, it is embedded deep in my mind, as anyone who ever rides with me in a vehicle as we cross into Nebraska will testify.

It's something about that sign, "Welcome To Nebraska," or maybe it's "Nebraska Welcomes You." Funny, I can't remember what the sign says, but I do know what the sign does to me. As soon as I see that sign, I am compelled to burst forth in song. Out of my mouth comes this song. It's not the prettiest of renditions, but the song does get sung, usually loudly, nasally, and a little flamboyantly! Hard to imagine, I know.

I suppose this started when we moved away from Nebraska when I was in eighth grade. We moved back to California, where I and all my siblings were born, but I am here to tell you, California wasn't Nebraska. No snow, little rain, and very few family members! It was a family desert as well as a real one. Suffice it to say that the first time we went "home" on vacation and crossed into Nebraska, we were just giddy enough to start this tradition. And why break with tradition, especially such a satisfying one?

Missing Grandma—Life Is Change

To every thing there is a season, and a time to every purpose under the heaven.

~ Ecclesiastes 3:1

JULY 2010

TODAY I MISS GRANDMA. IT'S not surprising, really. It is the end of July, and we are preparing for the biennial reunion in Broken Bow, Nebraska. It's natural that we should be especially conscious of the loss since Grandma went to heaven last fall, and this will be the first reunion without her. Oh, there will be plenty of evidence of her life. Over one hundred living, breathing evidences, actually. But, it won't be the same. Other years, Grandma and I would have started talking months ago about the reunion. She really lived those last few years in the anticipation of the next family event, the next birth of a great-grandchild. I've missed that. I've thought several times about those calls, wishing I could hear her say, "The reunion will be here again before we know it."

The reunion officially starts at noon on a Saturday; however, for most of us, the real beginning was dropping by to see Grandma— and Grandpa, when he was alive—when we got to town. First, it was at their house where you would find them hanging out on the porch, receiving their family. The yard would be full of people of all sizes. After Grandma went to the nursing home, the first stop would be her room. Sometimes it got so full we took turns. That's how it started.

The reunion officially ends after dinner Sunday, but a lot of people stay until Monday. The real end is when you say goodbye to Grandma. Many times there was another "traffic jam" as people stopped by Sunday night and Monday morning.

So, when does it start and end this year? I don't know. Maybe we need to have a new tradition. I guess we will adjust and go on; that's what life is, one change after another. This is one change, though, that I'm not really enjoying.

Maybe it's a little glimpse of what it will be like when we get to heaven. We'll want to see all of the family, but the first stop . . . that will be when we see Jesus. And the best part? There won't be a visit at the end where we have to say goodbye. And God will never say, like Grandma used to, "It's good to see them come, and it's good to see them go."

"The rapture could come at any moment. Eat dessert first!"

~ Grandpa McKnight

That All the Family Might Know

A FEW DAYS BEFORE HE died, I sat by Grandpa Jones' bed in the nursing home. He fiddled with the blankets, frustrated that his life was nearing an end. He wanted to be home. He wanted things to be as they used to be. The silence was painful for me, and since I don't believe in silence, I started the conversation with a question. "Grandpa, what was the favorite place you ever lived?"

Without hesitation, he answered, "Survey Valley."

I wasn't surprised. The Survey Valley is in the Sandhills of Nebraska, north of Ashby. It is the place they moved to, by covered wagon, in 1913. Grandpa was eight. He grew up there, he married and started his family there, and his heart never really left. He wrote about it in his books—the people and the places.

From 1978-2005, the places I lived in Wyoming, Nebraska, and South Dakota all led to a frequent traveling of Highway 2 through the Sandhills to get to Grandpa and Grandma's. Even now, when we  travel from the Carolinas to Rapid City, we travel via Highway 2 most of the time, just from the opposite direction. So indirectly, I have developed a love of the Sandhills. It feels like home. It is the place of my roots. Daddy was born in this sod house in the Sandhills during the Depression. My dad's older brother, Jim, is the boy in the picture.

I remember once, when I was about seven, the family made a trek one Saturday up to the site of the old sod house. It wasn't there anymore. If I remember right, we found some foundations on the property and an old garbage dump. What I remember most about that day was the feeling that pervaded the air. It seemed everyone was a little excited mixed with sadness. Everyone wanted to see the place where . . .

This kind of visit is so important in this day and age of comfort and ease. Oh, I know the economy is bad and people are struggling. But—seriously, folks—have any of you lived in a sod house? (Daddy and Uncle Jim, put your hands down.) Did you have to use cow chips for fuel? I think it is important for children and adults alike to hear the stories of the past so they can see not only how good we have it but also the many ways God took care of those who came before us.

It reminds me of a story Daddy used to tell when he was preaching from the Old Testament book of Joshua. The Israelites made a monument of the rocks they picked up as they crossed the Jordan on dry land. It was so their descendants would remember what God had done. We all need monuments.

> *When your children shall ask their fathers in time to come saying,*
> *What mean these stones? Then ye shall let your children know, saying,*
> *Israel came over this Jordan on dry land. For the LORD your God*
> *dried up the waters of Jordan from before you until ye were passed over*
> *as the LORD your God did to the Red Sea, which he dried up from*
> *before us, until we were gone over: That all the people of the earth*
> *might know the hand of the LORD, that it is mighty: that ye might*
> *fear the LORD your God forever.*
> ~ Joshua 4:21-24

No Fear

O magnify the LORD with me, and let us exalt his name together. I sought the LORD, and he heard me, and delivered me from all my fears.

~ Psalm 34:3-4

I HEARD THIS WEEKEND THAT forty percent of our personalities are due to our "raising." I find that interesting. I don't know how on earth they came up with those figures, but I can tell you that I believe with all my heart that events in our childhood do change us.

For instance, I know that my mother's death when I was ten forever changed who I was. How can it not? I have long believed that my fear of sudden bad change relates directly to that event. Trauma. It changes us.

However, I see in my nieces and nephews—some very much like their Aunt Miriam—the same dislike for conflict, the same fear of bad change. I see it when we watch movies or when they hear a story. I don't believe it is more than the norm, but there must be some of that in the sixty percent that is their genetic makeup. Of course, I hope that they get through childhood without anything happening to accentuate that tendency.

Or do I?

I know that I struggle as a Christian with trusting God. I got a new coffee mug this weekend and it says TRUST on it! I am managerial (aka bossy), and I like to be in control. I don't want to let go because what if the worst-case scenario happens? I think maybe, just maybe, I can help God. If I must admit it, what I am really saying in my heart of hearts is . . . I think I can do a better job than God. Well!

Hell-o-o-o-o-o, Miriam.

This summer, God put a situation in my life I'd never even thought to fear. It was so far beyond the realm of what I dreamed up that it hit me like a train out of nowhere. I can't fix it. Only God can.

I am helpless in myself. I have no answers other than those that come from God. But you know what? God has been pouring HIS help from heaven like He's taken the fire hose, aimed the nozzle at me and my family, and opened it up full-blast. He has shown me that HE has the power, HE has the mercy, HE has the love, HE has the justice, HE has the knowledge. I am the vessel, nothing more, nothing less. HE'S GOT IT!

So this weekend, I went to a conference. I thought I was there to learn how to be more professional in my speaking opportunities. HA!

Oh, that was part of it. I learned a lot. But, what God really did was in my heart. He showed me through listening to other amazing stories of the power of God on the lives of these thirty-one women that He has IT! He showed me that if I keep my focus on Him, I can overcome any barrier Satan would like to put in my path.

And then I thought He was done.

On the last morning, we took a photo. As I sat on a staircase surrounded by my new friends, God spoke to my heart. He reminded me of all of the things He has done the past few months. He reminded me of the verses He gave me just at the moment I needed them. He reminded me of the breakthrough I experienced the night before. He reminded me that He has IT.

As I stood up, this new thought flew through my brain. I have no reason to be afraid. None.

It was such a simple moment. No tears. No drama. No thunder or lightening. Just the still, small voice of God turning the key of change in my heart.

This morning as I woke up, I prayed, Lord, this day is yours. Do with it what you want.

Oh, I've prayed that before, but it was always followed by moments of terror over what HE would do to me since I'd been so foolish as to ask HIM to control MY day. Today, it was followed by peace.

And that's when I knew that God did something to that forty percent of my personality. Oh, I'm sure the sixty percent hereditary inclination to managerialness and fear will still jump up to try and grab back control. But I have something now I didn't. I have confidence in the safety of trusting the God who "has it!"

So for my nieces and nephews—I can't bring myself to pray that their lives will be pain free. But, I will pray that their hearts will be tender to face each trial knowing that God HAS IT—and them—firmly in His grip!

Section 5

A Legacy of Memories

Cowboys in the Park

IT'S NOT LIKE I WAS hurting for something to do last Friday. I had a huge list of tasks that needed accomplished and a class for work on Saturday, so I really needed to stay home and put my nose to the grindstone.

However, once I saw the notice in the paper that the concert in the park downtown was cowboy music, I knew there was nothing on the list that couldn't wait—or wouldn't have to.

When I got to the park, I couldn't believe my eyes. There were cowboy hats in the town square. Cowboy hats on people wearing jeans and cowboy boots. I could feel my heart rate jump. I picked a park bench close to the microphones. I wanted to hear every word.

Oh my. For the next hour, I sat and alternately resisted the urge to jump up and twirl across the grass like a child unable to contain her joy, or sit and wail because I missed my family, especially my Grandpa Jones.

They sang a lot of the old cowboy songs, and the crowd sang along. I heard comments about memories from the picture show when they were children. My memories were a bit different.

I remembered helping Grandpa saddle Penny, the horse he kept for the grandkids to ride. I remembered riding with Grandpa to get some cows in and having my glasses knocked off my face when

I failed to see a branch. I remembered watching hours of the old westerns on TV on Sunday afternoons at Grandpa and Grandma's ranch. They all paraded through my head.

When they sang a song by "Grandpa Jones" from the *Hee Haw* TV show, I laughed because my Grandpa Jones loved watching that show. When they sang a song that asked where the cowboys have gone, I wanted to stand up and shout, "THEY ARE STILL THERE!"

I thought of my cousin, riding across the Sandhills of Nebraska on his horse as he works his ranch. I wished every one of those people there could see a real cowboy, on a real ranch. I felt like I knew something they didn't know. I felt blessed.

It was cool, and there was a chilly breeze. If I closed my eyes, I could imagine myself in Nebraska or South Dakota. By the middle of the concert, I was shivering, but I certainly wasn't going to get up and go anywhere.

I was right where I wanted to be, enjoying an evening in Nebraska and South Dakota in downtown Newberry, South Carolina!

Picture Power

"Somehow I ended up with all of the pictures."

~ Grandma Jones

ONE OF THE FIRST THINGS I did every time I went to Grandpa and Grandma Jones' house was pull out the photo albums. I couldn't get enough of looking at those pictures.

When Grandpa Jones died in 1998, Daddy was in Chicago with my brother at a meeting. Mom and I headed on to Broken Bow, and Daddy met us there while my brother went home to get his family. So, for the two days before the funeral, I was the only grandchild there with all of the children, their spouses, and Grandma. They were two of the best days of my life. Besides listening to stories, I got to help sort pictures.

We sat and looked through boxes of photos. Grandma sat in her chair and watched. Whenever one of her children couldn't identify a photo, she would give it a whirl. Then we would carefully write the names on the backs of the picture.

At one point, she shook her head and said, "Somehow I ended up with all of the pictures." She was right. Often, when someone in the family died, they brought the pictures to her house. She had a lot of pictures.

I can relate. I had a lot of pictures that I brought into our marriage. They were mostly from the ten years of "aunthood." I have pictures of every birthday, every lost tooth, every everything for the oldest nieces and nephews up until the time I got married.

Shortly after I got married, we inherited my husband's family home. It came with a lifetime of belongings and memories. It turns out that his mother "somehow ended up with all the pictures" too. Or, at least, it seems that way. We've found a couple of boxes of photos, and some still need to be identified. I love to pull them out and have Bruce tell me who they are. One of these days, we'll have his aunt come over and help us identify more.

Why are these pictures so important? Last December, my daddy turned eighty. For his birthday, I put together a "This Was Your Life" slide show. As Daddy and I sorted through pictures, he brought up stories I'd never heard. He showed me the last picture ever taken of my mother. He explained why she looked so tired—it was taken at the end of a long day.

I found one of me and my sister, sitting on tiny children's chairs at our grandparents' house one Christmas. I now have one of those chairs at my house.

In old pictures, I saw the faces of some of my nieces and nephews in the faces of my parents and siblings when they were younger, and I thrill at the way God passes genetic similarities from generation to generation.

I think pictures are important because they tell us our history. We can see where we came from. They also put the present into perspective. Looking at pictures of that sod house, I realize I have it pretty good! They show us the potential of our future. Grandma never imagined when she married Grandpa that she would end up with that many pictures of new babies, birthdays, graduations, and weddings.

Photos are important pieces of who we are and who we can become.

Maybe you have a box at your house. Get that older generation together soon. Don't wait for someone to die. Let them sit around with coffee or tea and argue about whose baby that is! And you? You can sit back and listen! Or better yet, you can write the names on the backs of the photos.

Watermelon Memories

WE BOUGHT A WATERMELON THIS evening. Yummo! I tell you what—there is nothing that spells SUMMER better than a good watermelon. I can't buy watermelon without thinking of Grandpa Jones and the amazing melons he used to grow in Central Nebraska. Oh my. When it was a good year, we were eating melons with every meal and for snacks. You couldn't eat them fast enough. We actually were staying there one fall when they had an especially productive year. I almost—not quite, but almost—got enough.

That reminds me of another fun memory I have in regard to watermelon. The summer of 1973, we were spending our week out at the ranch, and Grandpa took us over to Uncle Jim's place for the day. They were going to a 4-H meeting and invited us along. At the 4-H meeting was a truck full of watermelons, and the adults kept cutting watermelon as the kids kept eating. Somehow my cousin Vernon, his friend, and I got into a who-can-eat-the-most-water-melon contest.

I am quite proud to say I won! I ate thirteen and a half pieces of watermelon, and the contest ended not because we were done but because they ran out of watermelon. My cousin ate twelve pieces, and I can't remember how many his friend ate. Judging from how I felt after eating one large piece tonight, I would NOT be able to repeat that performance today.

The next spring when Daddy had us write a letter to our new mom-to-be, I wrote about my watermelon eating feat. At eleven, I apparently felt this was an accomplishment she needed to know about. She wrote back and told me that, while she had never eaten that much watermelon, she had eaten so much ice cream in one sitting that it almost made her sick. With that one acknowledgement, my new mother won my heart. I still remember the feeling that she did indeed understand me. She was a kindred spirit.

I am proud to say that I was right. There are not enough words in this world to express exactly how much her coming to our home meant to me. She set things right in so many ways in my life and in our little family. I am so thankful for God's ability to give us exactly the people we need in our lives. She has become one of the best friends I could have.

So maybe it's not so much the watermelon I'm enjoying, although the taste is hard to beat. Maybe it's the special people who have colored the tapestry of my life.

Making Sensible Sense of Senses

THIS MORNING I AM GOING to a Christian school to speak to their students about writing. I am very excited. The lower grades will hear a presentation about my path as an author, interwoven with educational information about the writing process. The older students, though, are going to be hearing about senses. They may even be using their senses to do some writing of their own.

Why did God give us senses? Well, of course it was so that we can taste our food, smell the flowers, feel when things are injured, see where we are going, and communicate through speech. Simple.

But there is more to it than that. I believe one of the most important reasons is so we can create and recall memories.

Let me explain.

This morning I woke up with Grandpa McKnight on my mind. It might be because the pastor of the church school I'll be visiting today used to be Grandpa's pastor. It also might be because I'm going to speak on the senses, and I've been reminded of him several times this week through my own senses.

I made pot pie this week. Every time I eat pot pie, I remember Grandpa. It starts with the sight of the steaming pan with that flaky brown crust on top. Then the smell smacks me in the face, and I'm right back in Grandpa's kitchen with him. He liked making pot pies to put in the freezer for some evening when he had no idea what to fix for him and Grandma to eat.

But, the first thing that set me off this week was ironing some of my husband's shirts. Now, I know they are permanent press, but unfortunately our dryer doesn't always get them just how we want them. Besides, I enjoy ironing. Not only does it give me great satisfaction to see the end result, it employs my senses.

When I iron, I love the feel of the smooth cloth under my hand. I love the warmth that radiates up from the material. I have random memories pop into my head when the smell of the warm cloth reaches nose: memories of my mother ironing all of those cotton dresses and shirts, all damp from being sprayed, rolled, and tucked in the laundry basket to wait their turn; and memories of Grandpa McKnight.

When I was in my 20s and 30s, I would go visit my grandparents in Georgia. I would travel down, spend a week, and help Grandpa as much as I could. Grandma was an invalid and unable to leave her room very often. Even with the help of his daughters, it was a heavy load for Grandpa. I would iron some shirts and his huge handkerchiefs. I would cook some food ahead, and we would put it in the freezer. Grandpa would tell me stories. Repeatedly.

He would start with stories about his childhood. Then he would go on to his teenage years and the first jobs he worked. He would tell me about meeting Grandma, getting married, raising a family. He was an awesome story teller. Then, I would go home.

When I returned, he would tell them all again. After the second or third time through the Conservative Baptist Convention in Denver story, I realized something. Since I knew he wasn't senile, there was only one reason he kept repeating his stories. He wanted someone to remember them. He didn't want them to die with him. So, the next time I arrived, I pulled out the cassette tapes I'd brought and stuck one in his tape recorder. "Grandpa, I want you to start at the beginning again. I want to tape it all."

As I cooked chicken pot pies, he talked about how much he regretted not appreciating his stepdad more and about the impact of the persistence of his Sunday school teacher on his life and ministry. As we sat in their living room, he spoke of the Depression and sleeping by the stove in the kitchen because all of the bedrooms were full of other family members needing a place to stay. And as I ironed, he once again told me about the church convention in Denver, the one where the votes were so close they finally asked people to refrain from going to the restroom until all of the voting was over!

That time when I left, I took a treasure with me. A treasure for my Grandpa. His stories were safe. A treasure for me. I can pop a tape in and hear his voice. A treasure for the entire family, since my cousin transcribed all of the tapes onto the computer and put them on CDs for us.

How about your memories? Are you using your senses to their full potential? Why don't you write down the memories that pop into your head today? If you don't write, tape them. Or better yet, sit down with a child or young person and tell the story. Repeatedly!

Fifty Miles of Elbow Room

WHEN I WAKE UP EACH morning here in North Carolina, I first look out the window. It's a habit I developed when we first started making the long trip up from South Florida. I loved that I could lie in bed, look out the window, and see nothing but nature. No people, only trees, more trees, and sky. It seems like every morning is a new experience. Right now, the leaves are so beautiful. The vibrant oranges, yellows, reds, and even some greens are all fighting for attention. Without my glasses on, it looks like an Impressionist painting. I love Impressionist art.

My husband is often up before I am. Not infrequently, he makes coffee for me so the smell of coffee wanders into the bedroom. On Sundays, he sometimes turns on the radio to a program of Christian bluegrass music. It takes me right back to mornings at the ranch when Grandpa would turn on the radio (country music out there), and the smell of coffee and Grandma's breakfast would be wafting around the house.

This morning, it was all happening at once. Then I heard a song I'd never heard before. It is called "Fifty Miles Of Elbow Room." "Sounds like Wyoming to me," I said.

"Or the Sandhills," added Bruce. No doubt!

I love the way God gave us our senses. We get to enjoy all of

His beautiful creation, and then somehow those smells, sights, and tastes all hide themselves in our brains, and when we least expect it, one of them triggers a memory from long ago. I'm thankful for each and every memory and for the senses God gave me to remember them with.

Of course, the song was talking about the hereafter and all of its spaciousness. A friend commented on the beauty found in the Appalachian Mountains right now. Her thought was this: if a fallen earth is so beautiful, imagine what heaven will be like. Wow. I wonder if we will get to sleep in heaven. I would love to wake up each morning, open my eyes and see . . . well, I can only imagine.

I've Looked at Books from Both Sides Now

OUR PROJECT FOR THE DAY involves emptying a bookcase and sorting through the books to determine which ones are to be kept or given away. Note I didn't say "thrown away." We don't do that with books.

This bookshelf was built by Bruce's daddy to hold the encyclopedias they bought for their boys. Their children were going to have an education. So, it won't be discarded. It will be given to one of his brothers, or we will keep it.

The problem is that we have boxes of our own books waiting for space. And, if you ventured into our home in Newberry, you would see rows and rows, shelves and shelves of more books.

However, we don't like getting rid of books, even if we are only giving them away. I'm guessing the books we sort today will go into boxes and be stored, for now. Maybe forever.

We like books. We come by it naturally.

After all, the first project we undertook at this house—after placing dehumidifiers—was to remove the approximately five thousand paperbacks from the front room. Yes, I said five thousand.

We took the majority to the Friends of the Library, a couple of boxes to a friend in Florida, and kept a few. There was a handful that were so torn and ruined that we burned them in the garden. Gulp. I almost deleted that last sentence. It was sad.

If you went to my parents' house, you would also see a lot of bookshelves. Daddy has perfected the art of making bookshelves out of cement blocks and lumber. It's easy to take down and move, easy to put up, and it works.

Anyway, today we must move the bookshelf in order to remove a carpet. Then, realistically, the time is now to sort and decide.

So, what are we doing now? Bruce is working on his computer, and I'm typing this piece. We are procrastinating.

We've fortified ourselves with sausage gravy and biscuits, I've enjoyed my coffee, and I even put on my green 1996 Jones Family t-shirt for comfort. It reminds me of Grandpa Jones, who believed in saving things because you might use them someday. Wait, this might not be the shirt to use . . .

Ingles, the Love of God, and "Be Still My Soul"

Be still and know that I am God. I will be exalted among the heathen,
I will be exalted in the earth.

~ Psalm 46:10

WHAT DO THE INGLES GROCERY store, God's love for us, and "Be Still My Soul" have in common? Nothing to anyone else, I'm sure, but to me they add up to this: I miss Grandpa McKnight this weekend.

On Friday, I went to Ingles grocery just down the road. The first time I ever went to an Ingles, I was with Grandpa. It was his favorite grocery store in Athens, Georgia, where they were living. When I came to visit, we would go get groceries on occasion, and going anywhere with Grandpa was always an experience. He was full of sayings, some funny, some wise, some pithy. One thing I remember from Ingles was when he bent down in the parking lot to pick up a penny. He looked at me and said, "Susie, if you are ever too rich to stop and pick up a penny, you are too rich."

He would banter with the clerks who all knew him—always polite but, my, he did love to tease. Every time the clerk would announce how much he owed, he would hesitate a few seconds, then he would smile at her. "I think I can pay that today," he would say. She would smile back, charmed by the repetition of a joke, like old friends who know what you are going to say, but enjoy it anyway.

A few minutes ago, when I turned some music on, the song that came up first was "Oh, How I Love Jesus." Grandpa McKnight was strong on the love of God. He never got over the fact that God loved him enough to send Jesus to die for him, and it showed. It showed in the way he preached, often on that topic. It showed in the glow he got on his face when he lifted it toward heaven in prayer. He showed it in his care of Grandma and his family. Even his advice was always seasoned with love. I miss that. I could use some of his advice this week. There are things I would love to discuss with him. I'd sacrifice ice cream for the rest of my life to be able to sit and discuss things with him again.

Yesterday someone posted a verse about "Be Still My Soul" on Facebook. I have this habit of phrases and words setting off music in my head. I like to say there is a song for every occasion, and the one that popped into my head was the song with that same title. The words were written in 1752 by Katharina von Schlegel and the music in 1899 by Jean Sibelius.

> Be still, my soul: the Lord is on thy side.
> Bear patiently the cross of grief or pain.
> Leave to thy God to order and provide;
> In every change, He faithful will remain.
> Be still, my soul: thy best, thy heavenly Friend
> Through thorny ways leads to a joyful end.

Be still, my soul: thy God doth undertake

To guide the future, as He has the past.

Thy hope, thy confidence let nothing shake;

All now mysterious shall be bright at last.

Be still, my soul: the waves and winds still know

His voice Who ruled them while He dwelt below.

This song was sung at Grandpa's funeral. Or maybe it was at Grandma's. I don't remember for sure, but I always associate this song with Grandpa. It is such a majestic song with such comforting words. Grandpa was the best bear-hugger I ever met, and this song makes me feel like I'm getting a big bear hug from God. In a way, the fact that this scriptural advice in song reminds me of Grandpa helps. Through a song I associate with him, I receive the advice I need right now.

Be still. Know that God is God. He will take care of things. He has a plan. He is faithful. I can be confident. I am safely in His hands.

"I have four daughters. Rather than trying to remember which name I wanted, it was easier to just call 'Susie.' Then they all come! It works for granddaughters too."

~ Grandpa McKnight

Soundtrack of My Childhood

WHEN I WAS A CHILD, our home was always filled with music. My mother came from an extraordinarily musical family, and she was certainly one of the best. She could play the piano like nobody's business, and she could sing. Her solo voice was "discovered" when she went to college and took voice lessons.

The story goes that she didn't tell her parents she was singing a solo in the Christmas concert, and when she stood and sang "O Holy Night" in her clear, un-warbling soprano, Grandpa cried so hard the pew shook. This was his form of high commendation.

Daddy is not musically talented. He has a beautiful speaking voice but struggles with hearing his note. However, he determined, along with my mother, that they would fill their home with music. He felt that if there had been more music in his home when he was a young child, he might have developed an ear for music. So he bought music.

They signed up for a record club. Over several years, they received a pretty good batch of records. There were some from the Ralph Carmichael Orchestra and the Ralph Carmichael Singers. There was one from the Revivaltime Radio Choir. We heard the White Sisters. Over the years as opportunity arose, they added to the record stash, and it now includes George Beverly Shea and Jim

Reeves, among many others.

One of my favorite memories is being allowed to choose which records would go in the stack on the little record player. In fact, when we were sick, our day consisted of camping out on the couch and manning the record player. There were several story records from the Children's Bible Hour and Ethel Barrett, and one about Johnny Appleseed and Paul Bunyan. Of course, the story ones were played first, but then when you were tired, you would put on a stack of music and drift off to sleep.

Recently, we've enjoyed the opportunity to listen to some of these records again. I turn them on and go about my work. I listen to them as I fall asleep at night. Peace descends on my soul like a Grandma's quilt on a cold day. It is like hot chocolate for my soul. Even though it's been fifteen years since I last heard any of them, I find myself knowing the next song before it starts.

This is the soundtrack of my childhood.

I wonder, in homes across America, what is the soundtrack of childhood for the youth of today? Is it ABC, CBS, NBC, MTV, FOX, CNN, American Idol? My soundtrack involves old hymns sung in old styles. Most people would say it is outdated. It certainly is dated in some ways.

But, it is my soundtrack, the soundtrack of a joyful home where Christ was the reason for every season of life, and I am thankful beyond words.

Grandma and the Orange Acorn Squash

I'M NOT A GARDENER, BUT I'm learning. I've enjoyed playing at it off and on through the years. When I had space, I liked to grow a few things. I always plant tomatoes and cucumbers because, of course, a person needs a cucumber-tomato sandwich once in a while. I also love the squash family, especially acorn squashes.

I shared this love for acorn squashes with Grandma Jones. About ten years ago, I grew a little garden in my backyard in Rapid City. I planted the usual things—including the squash—and decided to grow some pumpkins too. I love pumpkin pie and pumpkin bars. Yummy.

As my little garden grew, I kept Grandma Jones informed of the progress of the growth, especially of the acorn squash. I promised her that when I came in the autumn to see her, I would bring her some.

She was delighted. Every time I called, she would ask how the garden was doing. I would tell her the latest woes or successes, but always, always I would make sure she knew how the squash was coming.

Towards fall, I started noticing an oddity—a problem with the acorn squash. They were turning kind of orange. It was an odd color for acorn squash, but they looked fine otherwise. I commiserated with Grandma; she thought it strange too.

Finally, the day arrived when I made my trip to Nebraska to see Grandma. I proudly pulled out the acorn squash in all of its orangeness, and I showed it to Grandma. She raised her eyebrows but didn't say anything as I recall. I baked it like she wanted it, and we ate it with dinner. It was good with a bit of butter and salt but tasted different somehow, not quite like the acorn squashes I was used to.

After we finished eating, Grandma looked at me and said, "Miriam, I think your acorn squash is a pumpkin!"

Well. So I'm here to tell you that you can eat a pumpkin like an acorn squash.

This year as I planted the garden in North Carolina, I remembered this problem. I was bound and determined not to repeat the mistakes of the past. I would NOT forget where I planted things. I would write them down. So, I pulled out a sheet of drawing paper. As we planted, I would write on the paper what and where it was. That paper soon became creased, folded, and even dirty after many trips out to the garden.

Just the other day, I took it out to see if I could identify some of my little plants. Bruce made labels for most of the main areas, which he laminated and put on stakes, but the squashes, pumpkins, and melons weren't labeled yet. I stuffed the paper in my pocket when I was done and proceeded to weed.

A couple of days later, I went looking for the paper but couldn't find it. I figured in all of the mess of construction/gardening, it was simply mislaid. I figured it would show up. It did.

After doing a load of laundry, I pulled our shirts out of the washer. There was a layer of white linty stuff all over the shirts. Something I didn't recognize. "What is that?" Bruce asked.

"I don't know," I said. But, over the next twenty-four hours, I began to wonder. My jeans were in that load too. I reached into the jeans pocket, and out came a stamp-sized paper. It was the map of my garden—or what was left of it. Oh dear. I think I can hear Grandma laughing in heaven.

Fortunately, I know where the pumpkins are, and I know where the acorn squashes are. I've wondered if my original pumpkins and squashes cross-pollinated, so this time I planted them on opposite sides of the garden. But, the yellow squash and green squash—those I'm not too sure of!

Memory Soup

TONIGHT I MADE CREAM OF acorn squash soup for the first time. Now, it might not sound very good to you but it was—good, that is.

It kind of surprises me that I would enjoy such a thing. It seems like "frou-frou" food to me. But, then I do like soup. I like acorn squash too.

As I stood at the counter this evening, scraping the baked squash out of the skins, I smiled. Grandma Jones would have enjoyed eating some of this squash. She loved acorn squash. It was her favorite.

I grinned again when I thought about the mix-up between pumpkins and acorn squash, but that's a story I already told. Tonight it wasn't going to be acorn squash. It was going to be acorn squash soup.

I would need my old Betty Crocker Picture Cookbook.

That's when I began to realize this was going to become a collision (collusion?) of memories! You see, more people are involved in this soup-making.

When I was little, Mommy always used the Betty Crocker Picture Cookbook. Do you know the one? Hers was a hard back copy. It has a red and white cover. It came out in the 50s and was reprinted a few years ago. Well, my older sister got our mother's, and I always wanted one for myself. So, one day when I was visiting Grandma McKnight down in Athens, Georgia, I mentioned how much I wished I could find one of those cookbooks. Grandma decided right then and there that I would have hers. And so I do. It's even better since it's in a three-ring binder.

But, it was Mom who told me about the recipe. A couple of years ago, she asked, "Have you ever used the cream soup recipe from the Betty Crocker Cookbook?" I assured her I hadn't. She said that she tried it with some left over celery and they really enjoyed it. So, I took her suggestion—only I used asparagus. That's the beauty of the recipe. You can use any vegetable, really. You just need one cup pureed vegetable of your choice and, *Voilà!*, there you have it.

Tonight I served it with oyster crackers. They are the ones I bought the other day purely because they remind me of Grandpa and Grandma Onstott. That's the first place I ever remember seeing them. I thought they were amazing and fancy.

So, today I ate delicious cream of acorn squash soup, and it reminded me of six of the most important people in my life: my mother, Grandma Jones, Grandma McKnight, Mom, and Grandpa and Grandma Onstott. Now that's a recipe for comfort food!

Section 6

Legacy of Affirmation

The Power of a Story

THE TOPIC CAME UP THIS morning as we were getting ready for church. Somehow, in our conversation, a much-repeated phrase popped out.

"There'll be no smilin' on this bus." We both laughed at a reference to a funny statement made by Bruce's niece some twenty-five-plus years ago.

"She'll never live that one down," Bruce said.

I don't think she really minds. It's a sweet story that her daddy and uncles like to tell. It shows the adoration they all have for the little girl become young woman. What's not to like about that?

As I pondered the value of this story in the Bradley family, one of my own popped into my head. I shared it with Bruce. I remember Grandma Jones telling this story several times. She had a dry, quiet wit. When she told a story, you listened.

She recounted that when I was three or four, and we came to visit the ranch, I stood outside the hog pen. I watched. I listened. Then I proceeded to say with some disdain, "Pigs don't say oink."

When Grandma told the story, she would always laugh. I remember the glow and the feeling of love and security that always came with the telling.

It's a simple story. I've heard funnier ones. But, the thing that was so breathtakingly remarkable to me was the fact that my grandma, with twenty-three grandchildren, remembered that story and liked it enough to tell me and everyone around me. She delighted in a memory of me. She thought I was funny. She loved me for me!

What a powerful gift for her to give me. The gift of validation. The gift of love. The gift of a cute story!

This is a gift I can give to my nieces and nephews and all of those children with whom I come in contact. I can build them up not by approving the things they do, but by approving the person God made them to be—quirky personalities and all.

And this, folks, is why I tell stories!

Walker, Texas Ranger, and My Grandma

LATELY ONE OF THE LOCAL stations has been showing reruns of *Walker, Texas Ranger*. I've seen several of them. A lot of reruns are new to me since I never saw them when they first ran. Not Walker, though I knew about him. Not because I was watching it on TV, either. At least not at my house.

Grandma McKnight was a sweet, godly Christian, a pastor's wife who was a talented musician. She taught me to love the Psalms. She was a prayer warrior who spent night after night praying instead of sleeping because of pain. She counseled many people. She was a very gifted speaker.

She loved *Walker, Texas Ranger*.

What? Yep, it's true. One day when I was visiting, Grandma called to me from her room where she was bed-bound. "Miriam, come watch this with me." I could hear the excitement in her voice.

When I entered the room, she was propped up on her bed, her eyes twinkling. Her hands were trembling with excitement. "Miriam, I know this is a violent show, but I love it. This man has the fanciest footwork you would ever see." I looked at her, bemused. Was this my grandma?

148

I watched with her, and she became quite animated when Walker inevitably saved the day with his "fancy footwork." After the show, Grandma told me a bit more of her life story.

"When I was a child," she began, "I loved anything to do with music or rhythm. I wanted to learn to dance. My father didn't think I should dance, so he encouraged me to learn the organ. He felt that the pedals would give me the opportunity to use my feet in rhythm and satisfy that need." She smiled at me. "He was right."

So, whenever I see *Walker, Texas Ranger,* I watch because I like seeing the good guy win. I watch because it actually is one of the less violent shows on TV these days, and I watch because every time I see that "fancy footwork," I remember Grandma McKnight and the wisdom of her father.

"Miriam, I know this is a violent show, but I love it. This man has the fanciest footwork you would ever see."

~ Grandma McKnight

No Pain, No Gain

Whatsoever thy hand findeth to do, do it with thy might.

~ Ecclesiastes 9:10

PERSISTENCE IS AN IMPORTANT CHARACTER trait in life. I'm not sure I really have a lot of it. I have to be keenly interested in something to keep at it. Or I have to be afraid of disappointing others.

For instance, the piano. I love playing the piano, and I especially enjoy playing for church. God gave me the gift of a good ear for music. Without that, I wouldn't play like I do. Anyone who was around during the painful days of my childhood piano lessons and practice sessions could testify that I didn't have the discipline to become a good pianist. I wanted it to be easy. I didn't like hard things. I wanted it to be fun. In fact, I worked very hard every week to trick my mother into playing each song for me once. Then I could learn it mostly by ear. That certainly was easier and more fun for me than learning how to read the music.

When I was between fourth and fifth grades, I was introduced to the cello, which I instantly fell in love with. For some reason, it connected with me, and I would faithfully haul that instrument home with me every night to practice. Last month when we went to my niece's concert in South Dakota, I saw someone pulling a cello into the school in a hard case with wheels. Oh, what I wouldn't have given for one of those. I became pretty good on the cello, and my favorite class in junior high was orchestra.

When I was in eighth grade, tragedy struck. We moved to California. Now, the move wasn't the bad part. The bad part was that that my cello was a school instrument, and the school in California didn't have an orchestra, only a band—a marching band. My parents certainly didn't have the money to buy me a cello. Daddy understood my disappointment. I could tell he felt terrible, but he approached it with his practical wisdom.

"Miriam," he said, "the cello isn't very practical for church use in the long run. You really need to focus your talent on the piano. That can be used in so many different ways."

Right. I was less than thrilled with that idea. Much less.

So, I grudgingly started struggling through playing for Sunday school. I got so I could play a little. I wasn't very good, but it would do.

Fast-forward to my junior year in high school. We had moved again, this time to Gillette, Wyoming, and we were attending a small Christian school. The choir teacher was an enthusiastic lady who decided we were going to perform a cantata. She went to the local Bible book store and found a cantata reduced in price. She bought all of their copies and brought them to us.

She decided that since I was the best pianist in the bunch, I would play. When I looked at it, I nearly suffered a heart attack. This cantata was not straightforward hymns. It was arrangements. It had syncopation. (Timing wasn't my "thing"—remember my efforts to avoid reading music?) The pianist wasn't playing the melody all of the time. Instead, she would be bouncing her hands all over the piano. My hands didn't bounce.

"I can't play this," I shrieked in my usual mild, non-dramatic way.

"You have to. They are non-refundable." And that was that.

So, guess what? Somehow, motivation clicked in. People were depending on me. I didn't want to let them down or embarrass myself. I started practicing, measure by measure, song by song, until the book was memorized. I learned it, and in learning it, I discovered a love for the piano. It was an awesome cantata, and we did a great job. It was one of the high points of my high school years and has led to so many opportunities and hours of joy. Daddy was right . . . again.

Career Path by Grandpa

THERE IS ONE PARTICULAR ASPECT of my life right now that I am enjoying immensely. It involves my career. Well, let me correct that—my careers.

Two days a week, I work as a nurse on a general medical-surgical-oncology floor. Not being in the ICU anymore, I've enjoyed seeing more of my patients get well and go home. They are also more able to talk to me and share stories from their lives. Because of the population demographic here, most of the patients are elderly. I like old people. They are funny, wise, and often uninhibited in sharing their opinions. We get along well! However, they are sick people, and some of them are facing the realization that the end of their life is nigh.

It can be stressful.

My second career is that of writing-speaking. I have been spending an increasing amount of time visiting schools and speaking to students on the writing process and my path to

becoming an author. I am finally, really and truly using the elementary education degree I earned. Of course, you put me in front of a bunch of children, and I come alive. I am at my happiest speaking to children. It refreshes me to be in front of a whole group of living, breathing humans who have their whole lives in front of them.

It is relaxing and invigorating all at once!

So, you can see how I would think I have the best of both worlds. After all, I am a caregiver, and I am a teacher. That's who I am.

Isn't God grand?

There is also someone else who is particularly responsible for this dual career. That would be Grandpa Onstott.

Sometime around sixth grade, I got it into head that I wanted to be a nurse. I'm not sure why, but it lodged there, nonetheless. Unfortunately, this budding dream was squelched by the realization that I would pass out when painful things were discussed: for example, when the Sunday school teacher told us the crucifixion story. That is no lie—not even an exaggeration.

So, for the next six or seven years, I didn't even consider the possibility. Then . . . Grandpa took me hunting.

Now, he did teach me how to shoot, but mostly I was the noisy one that scared the deer his way. At any rate, we got a deer, and he took it home and hung it in the garage. After a few days, he said to me, "Miriam, you can come help me skin this deer."

Since it wasn't an offer or a question, I did it, and I survived. I won't say I enjoyed it. As I stood there watching, holding, and helping, this thought crossed my mind: If I can help skin a deer, I can be a nurse. Shortly thereafter, I enrolled in nursing school and it has been an amazing career for almost thirty years.

First, I obtained my LPN license. After a couple of years, I went back to school and earned an associate degree. I became an RN.

In 1991, I decided to take a break from nursing and go to a year of Bible college. It was something I always wanted to do, and now seemed to be the time. Why not? I was single with the ability to support myself while I did it, and my brother was attending a college I knew I would like. So I went. After a year, I realized that this was way too much fun, and I wanted to stay for more. The truth is that if I went to the moon and there were people there, I would make friends and want to stay. At any rate, I decided to stay. However, you could only take fun classes for one year without declaring a major. What major should I pick? I chose elementary education.

When I asked Grandpa Onstott for advice on this decision, he said something I'll never forget. "It never hurts to have more than one thing you can do, Miriam. That way, if one career path doesn't work out, you have another. The people who made it during the Great Depression were the ones who could switch gears because they had more than one set of skills."

So, there you have it: career path by Grandpa.

The Beginning

APRIL 16, 1905, MARKS THE beginning of my first book, *The Double Cousins and the Mystery of the Missing Watch*. Consequently, it marks the beginning of the Double Cousins Mystery Series!

On that day, my grandpa, George Lee Jones, was born in Kansas.

So you might ask, "What's the connection?" The obvious answer is that if he hadn't been born, I wouldn't have been born . . . but it goes farther than that, much farther.

When Grandpa was eight, his family moved from Kansas to Nebraska in a covered wagon. They went with two covered wagons, a spring wagon, eight horses, and six people. It was a cold October trip, taking sixteen days to go the approximate 320 miles. It was an experience he never forgot.

In fact, when he was in his seventies, he decided there were a lot of experiences he had that no one would remember if he didn't tell them. So he did. He not only told them, he wrote them down. He wrote three books about his life. He wrote simply but descriptively, using plain rancher talk. The books were full of wonderful examples of his dry sense of humor. I can read those books and still hear Grandpa talking in my head.

In December 1997 and January 1998, three of my grandparents

died in a six-week period. Grandpa Jones was the last one to go to heaven. Understandably, I was rather wrapped up in the memories I had of the things they taught me. My grandparents were all such an important part of my life, especially after Mommy died. Now there are grieving camps and counselors, etc., for children who suffer such loss, but when I was ten, there was only our wonderful daddy and our extended families, especially our grandparents. They were there for us, even from a distance. They stepped up and did what families are supposed to do.

When Daddy remarried, I got another set of grandparents. Through the years, these people were always there, teaching by example. There aren't enough words to express the effect they had on my life. Through this time of loss, I decided I wanted to take some of their stories, starting with Grandpa Jones's books, and put them into picture books for children. For instance, maybe a story from the covered wagon trip. That would make an awesome book.

As I started to study how to write a book, I learned that you should write what you know. That's where the idea came from for *The Double Cousins and the Mystery of the Missing Watch*. When I was a kid, one of my favorite places was the ranch. As a way of honoring my grandparents, I wanted to write about it. So I did.

So now you know why it is that I can say The Double Cousins Mysteries started in 1905.

If your grandparents are still living, go see them today or call them. Tell them how much you love them. Listen to them. They can tell you all sorts of intriguing stories and maybe, just maybe, it will inspire you to write something yourself!

My Biggest Fan

One of the primary reasons we decided to go ahead and publish the first book when we did was Grandma Jones. I felt the best

place to launch the book was in Broken Bow, Nebraska, at the county fair. It made sense, considering that's where part of the plot took place. The fair only happens once a year, the first week in August, and in December 2008, when we were considering this option, Grandma was 96. I desperately wanted Grandma to see the finished product since she IS the grandma in the book. She has also been my best and most constant encourager over the years. Almost every time I would call her, she would ask, "How is your book coming, Miriam?" She was excited when I gave her the rough draft shortly after finishing it, and she read it with great delight. So, when I realized that the chance of having another year at the fair with Grandma still around was not very likely, my husband and I decided to go for it.

Sure enough, after seven months of work, nail biting, and angst, the finished product came squeaking in just in the nick of time. We made it to the fair with the book in hand, and I was able to read some of it to Grandma. She was delighted to see it and hold it in her hands, even though she wasn't able to see it clearly or really concentrate on the book. She enjoyed all of the activity surrounding the book's launch too.

Last week, I went home for a book signing and to help Grandma celebrate her 97th birthday. She was in pain, tired, and frustrated with her inability to enjoy the day like she wanted, and we all hurt with her. Daddy had commented after the fair that God was still using her as a testimony to others, and she was bringing glory to Him through her thankful attitude even in the face of such a minimal "quality of life." He pointed out that when God's purpose for her was done, then He would release her to go to heaven.

Early this morning, God did just that. Grandma stepped into heaven. She sees perfectly now. She can walk, run, and express her thoughts clearly again. There is no pain. She is with Grandpa and all of the others who had gone on before her. And, most importantly, she is with Jesus. I am thankful that she was my grandma. I am thankful that she was such a godly lady, one who lived Proverbs 31:26. "She openeth her mouth with wisdom; and in her tongue is the law of kindness." I NEVER heard Grandma say anything unkind about anyone. I only wish that could be said about me.

I hope you have someone in your life who has been your example of a godly woman. I know I wouldn't be the person I am today without her influence. I will miss her desperately, but I am so glad she is finally home.

Hawking Memories at a Funeral

LAST MONDAY, WE GATHERED AGAIN in Broken Bow to say goodbye to Grandma. We came from three of the four corners of our country with the majority arriving from the Nebraska-Kansas-South Dakota area. We came, sad for our loss but so thankful Grandma wouldn't be suffering anymore. We cried, we laughed, we sang, we shared memories, we ate great food, and, oh yes, I sold books. Yes, I did. I admit it. I sold books out of the trunk of Daddy's car.

What??? How could you? Well, read my first book and you will understand. Or, at least, you may begin to understand. You see, it's a tradition.

My great-uncle, Ervin Jones, was known as Trader Jones. In the first book, I very creatively (hah!) called him Trader Johnson. He was called this for an obvious reason. His car trunk was always full of interesting stuff, stuff that someone would NEED. As in the book, he always showed up at the ranch with cowboy boots in various kids sizes so that we would have them to wear when we visited. Once, he even traded the hat right off his head. In the book, he is the one character who is completely recognizable. He would have been proud of me! Especially when I sold his granddaughter a book!

"But what about your grandparents?" you ask. Let me tell you about Grandpa Jones. When he was in his mid-seventies, he decided that he remembered a lot of things no one else did. He had memories that would soon be lost to everyone. So he wrote them down. He wrote three books over the next several years and self-published them. He then spent the rest of his life selling them or giving them away to anyone and everyone he came in contact with. He carried them around in his Bronco. I remember him selling them to people sitting beside him at rodeos, around town, anywhere he went. I'm pretty sure they were in his Bronco at a few funerals.

Then there is Grandma. Grandma was extremely proud of the fact that I was writing down some of our stories, stories that happened on their ranch. Stories that were from one of the best times of her life. Her life was hard, especially as a child and a young bride during the Depression. When someone commented to her about "the good old days," her response was, "They weren't that good." So once she and Grandpa started making a living on the ranch, it was easier to enjoy life. She loved having her children and grandchildren around. They were the best times of her life. Even up until her death, she always perked up when the children came into her room. She lived the last few years in anticipation of the next family reunion or gathering, when she would see all of the new babies.

So, while it may seem strange to an outsider that I would have books with me at the funeral, it seemed completely normal and expected. I didn't pull them out until someone asked for one. Then, no one blinked an eye. They grinned and told me I was turning into George Jones. I'd call that a compliment! They laughed and questioned if I was becoming Uncle Ervin. And they were glad I brought books. After all, why spend money on shipping if you don't have to? Oh, but that's another thing we learned from our grandparents: frugality!

Of Secrets and Kindred Spirits

"Keep writing."

~ Grandma Elizabeth Onstott

WHEN GRANDMA NAOMI ONSTOTT DIED, I spent the next al-most-year living with Grandpa and helping with the cooking and cleaning. I got a part-time job at McDonald's and went to the school of "Grandpa Onstott's wisdom." I listened as he shared memories of his life with Grandma. One evening over supper, he said, "My marriage with your grandma is like a book. It was beautiful, it was wonderful, but it is closed, and I can't ever open it again." I was the beneficiary of many lessons like this, shared through daily activities and experiences.

I also enjoyed a front row seat to the budding of his new love.

I remember when he sat at the supper table one Saturday night and told me what he planned for church the next morning. He was giddy—not normal behavior for this stoic German man—as he told me that he had asked Elizabeth McGee to marry him. I was privy to a huge, awesome, incredible secret. I knew before anyone else at church, and I couldn't tell. I COULDN'T TELL!

I hardly slept. In church, I sat in my spot, going through the motions of the service. I tried not to look at Grandpa since every time he caught my eye, I wanted to giggle, and he started to laugh.

Finally, at the end of the service, he dropped the bombshell. Everyone was delighted.

Grandpa's new wife, "Grandma Elizabeth," quickly became a dear friend and encourager. Over the years, she delighted me with her youthful outlook and love of laughing. I was amazed by her determination and strength through the difficult times in her life. Her joy was infectious, and she made Grandpa happy again. She was a kindred spirit.

She also believed strongly in me and my efforts. She was at my graduation from nursing school.

She was one of my biggest fans when I was writing the first book. I find it interesting in writing this, that two of my top fans were my grandmothers. Grandmas are awesome! But I digress.

When I called her to tell her I was engaged, she was so giddy with excitement she could hardly talk. When I sent her the first book, she was overjoyed and wrote me a letter I'll always treasure.

She was looking forward to the next book, even though she spent the past four months in the hospital struggling to breathe. I was excited for her to read this book, especially since part of the setting is her parents' farm near Lamar, Colorado. I never saw it, but I based the setting on descriptions she gave me and my own imagination.

She couldn't wait for the book, though. Her work here was done, and God called her home. Yesterday, she went to heaven and left behind the pain and the oxygen tubes. I bet her joyous laughter is ringing through heaven today.

She may have "only" been my step-stepgrandma, but she certainly was a good grandma to me. I'll miss her.

I can understand more and more why Grandpa McKnight was so anxious to get to heaven. All of my grandparents are there now. I miss them.

Section 7

Legacy of Common Sense

Security in a Pantry

ONE OF THE CHALLENGES TO getting settled here in Hendersonville has been the fact that we moved into the new addition before all of the finish work was done. We still didn't have pantry shelves or closet shelves when we moved in.

Bruce finished the pantry shelves yesterday just before I left for work. So, when I got home last night, I stood and admired the lovely empty space crying out to be filled. Today I had my chance.

Before going to work this afternoon, I transferred all of the pantry goods from the shelves in the "old kitchen" into the new pantry. I found my heart beating faster as I lined the cans up, all in good order. I love the look of all that food waiting to be used. Extra food makes me feel safe!

We both come from the same kind of background when it comes to stocking pantries. Our families weren't rolling in dough. Our parents kept food on the table and a roof over our heads. There was enough to eat. We were loved and safe. But, sometimes this required not only sacrifice but creativity!

Our moms watched the sales at the store. They bought in bulk when often-used items were on sale, and then those items were put aside for later. The lovely thing about this way of stocking a larder is that you always have something to fix. You even have a variety.

And like my sister said last year when her husband was out of work, "If the bottom falls out of your world and you have to live off what's in your pantry, you can."

When Daddy worked for a grocery store as a second job, he brought home the cans without labels that they were going to throw out. Sometimes we would open a can and eat the "mystery ingredient." It was kind of fun, an adventure. At least now, all of our food still has labels.

Bruce's mom worked at a grocery store, and during a period when business at the mill was bad and his dad was laid off a lot, she would bring home milk that had just expired and huge bags of unsweetened puffed wheat that she could get at a discount. Bruce was in college during the puffed wheat days, but his brothers remember it well.

When I organized the food from three pantries into one a couple of weeks ago, I told Mom what I'd done. "It helps sometimes to have to go through it all anyway," she said. "Then you know exactly what you have!"

She was right! I've even come up with some supper ideas from the forgotten foods in the pantry. There are others that have prompted me to find a new recipe.

The bonus to the whole process is that the cupboard shelves in the old kitchen, which were freed up, can now hold some of the extra dishes we brought with us until we can sort through and decide what we need to keep and what we can get rid of. I'm not holding my breath about that part, though. We don't just have pantry stockers in our family lines. We also have some keepers and savers.

She Lived . . . Stitch by Stitch . . .

She is not afraid of the snow for her household; for all her household are clothed with scarlet.

~ Proverbs 31:19

September 23, 2010

Last night I was exhausted—mentally, emotionally, and physically. So, I put myself to bed. I snuggled under my Grandma Jones quilt and drifted off to sleep.

Today is the 98th anniversary of the day Grandma Jones was born. This marks the first birthday we won't be celebrating with her. She is celebrating it in heaven, and I don't regret that. I miss her. A lot. But I know she was ready in every sense of the word, and I'm thankful she is there.

However, I couldn't help but think of the influence she had on the lives of so many people in this world. She wasn't famous. She wasn't rich. She wasn't a huge success by today's standards. Yet, in every way that really counts, she was famous, rich, and successful. And she did it stitch by stitch.

You see, Grandma Jones was a wife, mother, grandma, sister, friend, and daughter. She took her relationships and responsibilities seriously. One way she showed her care was by providing for her family. She made quilts—lots of quilts. When her children were at home, she made quilts to keep them warm. They weren't for show, although she loved to make them beautiful. As her family expanded, so did her quilt-making.

For each new grandchild, she made a baby quilt. There were twenty-three. For each grandchild's high school graduation, she made a tie-quilt. Yep, twenty-three. Then she went on to make each of us a quilt for a double bed. When she came to a wedding, she brought a quilt, and Grandpa brought money. A few years ago, when it became apparent even to her that she wouldn't be able to keep her house much longer, she gave out the quilts to those who weren't yet married. I put mine away for a while but then decided I wanted to use it, married or not.

Since getting married, I have kept the quilt folded at the bottom of the bed. When I'm cold, I pull it up. I can see different pieces of material in it that I recognize. They were remnants of things Grandma made for us when we were younger. I know that Grandma put a lot of love into each of the quilts she made, just like she put a lot of love into each of our lives.

Even though I don't have children, I can learn a lot from her. I need to use the talents I have to provide for and bless those God puts in my life. That's all He asks. I don't need to do it all at once, either. I can do it like Grandma, stitch by stitch, over a lifetime.

"If it won't matter in fifty years, it's not worth worrying about."

~ Grandma Jones

A Hurricane of Memories

RIGHT BEFORE OUR FIRST ANNIVERSARY, Bruce and I were sharing our favorite memories from that year. As I sorted through the mental pictures, one series kept coming back. There we were, in our backyard, under a tarp attached from under the eaves to poles in the yard. It was morning, and we were cooking coffee over a gas camp stove. Then it was night, and we were reading by lantern light. Then it was hot, midday, and I was canning little meatloaves in jelly jars on a gas camp stove . . .

What on earth?

Well, let me explain. The truth is that some of my best memories are related to the hardest experience of the year: Hurricane Wilma.

In preparation, we shuttered the house. We filled several two-liter bottles with water, just in case. We purchased many cans of tuna and corned beef. We filled all three vehicles with gas. Then we waited.

I was scheduled to be at the hospital on the "before-during" rotation. This meant that I was called in to the hospital the night before the hurricane started, and I would stay until it was over. They have people there to work the day shift, and then the night shift, so you bring your clothes, a book, your spouse or family, and there you are. Bruce decided to take them up on the offer, mostly to keep me happy, and we spent the night on an air mattress on the floor of a CCU room, listening to the wind howl through the shutters.

The hurricane hit early in the morning, more powerfully than expected. There were reports of funnel clouds in the storm, and we watched some of the shutters blow loose. Water came through windows, and part of the hospice department experienced roof damage from a major leak. The hospital staff pulled together and moved patients where needed until the storm stopped. We watched a tree fall on a car in the parking lot and breathed a sigh of thanks that it wasn't our car.

The storm abated about midday, and by the time I got off work, we were able to drive home. Traffic lights were down everywhere, some hanging down onto the ground in the middle of the intersections. There were whole rows of trees toppled, root ball and all, over on their sides. Huge evergreen trees looked like "the world's largest corncobs" as my husband said since all of their pine needles and branches were stripped off. When we rounded the corner onto our street, we were met with the sight we expected. The big tree in our front yard had toppled but, thankfully, into the street and not onto a house. Other than the tree, which tore up the entire front yard and a short stretch of fence, we suffered no damage. Kind neighbors had already cut the tree out of the street so that traffic could get in and out of our complex.

Through the next couple of weeks without power, we did what we had to do. We spent time reading, cooking up all of the meat thawing from the freezer, visiting with neighbors, and remembering how easy we have it these days. A couple days after the storm, I was at work when Bruce called. "Could we can that ground meat?"

"If we could find some canning jars, I'm sure we could," I said. "I know Grandma Jones canned meat. I'll ask around here at work and see if anyone knows where there is a store open that would sell them."

"Don't expect them to know what you are talking about," he said. He was right. I got nothing but blank stares when I asked if anyone knew where I could get canning jars.

One lady said, "If you want canned vegetables you go to the vegetable aisle at the store."

On returning home, I found that my husband's tendency to save things was proving helpful again. He went to the garage and dug out a box of brand new jelly jars, lids included, that he had bought to make jelly but never got around to it.

I called Grandma Jones, and she agreed it was worth a try. While she hadn't tried to can ground meat, she couldn't think of any reason why it wouldn't work.

So, for your information, you can process meat loaf by packing it into jelly jars, cooking it on a gas grill for one hour, heating the lids as for other foods, then processing in a pressure cooker on a gas camp stove for another hour. It comes out mushy, but it makes great meat loaf sandwiches.

Making Cheese . . .
A Good Idea or a Waste
of Good Milk?

I AM MAKING CHEESE. I have never made cheese before. I'm not sure yet if I'll ever make it again. There are two reasons I am making cheese.

My number one reason has to do with my impressionability factor. I read a book a couple of years ago with a chapter about making cheese. It sounded so easy, so delicious, so real-life-down-to-earth-back-to-basics that I knew I must try it. I really wanted to make mozzarella, but I couldn't find citric acid here in Newberry, and so I decided to make Neufchatel instead.

I now have a gelatinous mass of what looks like yucka-ucka sitting on the stove waiting to finish the gelling process. Yucka-ucka is the name a friend and I gave to a cheese and curd type mass that we were offered in Romania in 1994. We were offered yucka-ucka or fruit for dessert. We chose fruit.

The number two reason is that family cookbook I helped put together in 1998-2000. When we were at Grandma's house working on the cookbook, we raided her recipe box and books for favorite "Grandma recipes." We wanted recipes that she would have made when our parents were young. We found this recipe for a hard yellow cheese.

"This is the recipe I used all the time." Grandma peered at the card in her hand.

"It should go in the cookbook," someone said. We all nodded, delighted to have this piece of Grandma's history for our book.

Grandma lifted her eyes and looked at us in disbelief. It was almost like she was borrowing a phrase from Grandpa McKnight, only she was using her eyes to say it instead of her mouth. Her eyes said, "I thought my grandchildren were smarter than that." What came out of her mouth was "Why would you want to make cheese?"

"It's going in," we said. "Someone will want to try it."

"Well . . . I'm never making it again." Her voice was flat, matter-of-fact, and final.

So, over the years, I have commented many times that I wanted to make Grandma's cheese. I wanted to see what it tasted like. I wanted to see why she thought we were a bit touched to want to make cheese.

Today, not only is the yucka-ucka on the stove, but the rest of the very expensive (those two words were suggested by my husband) raw milk is on the counter clabbering (aka rotting, spoiling, going bad). This seems to be the first step to making Grandma's cheese. I'm beginning to understand.

Good Clean Dirt

He that tilleth his land shall be satisfied with bread: but he that followeth vain persons is void of understanding.

~ Proverbs 12:11

"One boy is a whole boy, two boys is half a boy, and three boys is no boy at all."

~ Grandpa Jones

HAVE YOU EVER REALIZED, LONG after the fact, how much someone sacrificed just because they realized it was beneficial to someone they loved? I have!

Grandpa and Grandma Jones were ranchers. That's how they made a living. It wasn't an easy life. It was serious work 24/7, 365 days a year. They weren't afraid of hard work, but they certainly knew how to work smart. They didn't purposefully do

things to make their work harder—except when it came to the children.

It was not unusual for several grandchildren to visit in the summer. Often, there were as many as seven visiting at the same time. I'm not sure why they did it that way. I've often thought maybe it was easier because we helped entertain each other. Or, maybe they wanted to foster the relationship between cousins. I'm sure those may have been two of the reasons, but I know one reason that it was not! It wasn't because it was less work for them. After all, one of Grandpa's favorite sayings was "One boy is a whole boy, two boys is half a boy, and three boys is no boy at all."

Grandpa had a lot of sayings. Some were spoken, some were just the way it was done. All of them were wisdom and character-building facts, rules for surviving the ranch experience.

Some of these sayings and lessons included things like, "Always wear boots when you ride a horse"—so you don't get dragged—and "Don't ever walk behind a horse"—so you don't get kicked. He always insisted we wear long pants when we were out in the pastures. You never knew when you would see a snake.

Grandpa Jones also used to say there was no shame in getting dirty as long as you got that way doing an honest day of hard work. He called it good, clean dirt. Every time I get filthy-dirty working hard, I think of Grandpa, and I know he would be proud!

Grandpa was a great source of wisdom on the benefits of hard work. I don't think many of us enjoyed cutting musk thistles. It was hot, dusty work, but it had to be done. We learned that too. Just because it is hard doesn't mean you quit.

A couple of years ago, Bruce watched my uncle get his 1931 Model A town car into the horse trailer he uses to transport it to parades. Bruce came away amazed at the determination and agility of the almost-eighty-year-old man. It was quite a scene of strength and contortionism to get out of the trailer after he had pulled the car in. There were only a few inches on each side of the car, so he had to climb backwards out of a window and slither along the side. When I told Daddy the story, he chuckled. "Our dad didn't teach us to give up just because it is hard."

Well, I guess not.

I know Grandpa recognized that having a bunch of us there at the same time wasn't always helpful. But he did it anyway. He realized that he had something to offer that his grandchildren needed to learn. He wanted to help his children have an impact on the next generation. And he did. We were expected to do our part and help with the chores, not only because we needed to learn the skill, but because that's what families do. And because it builds character.

I know for a fact that at least one grandchild was sent to the ranch for an entire summer because the words "I'm not the kind of kid who likes to work" escaped his mouth. So, off to the School of Grandpa Jones' Work Ethic he went. The thing was, he didn't think it was punishment. He loved the ranch. He loved helping Grandpa. And he learned to work.

That's the beauty of the situation. Even while making his life harder, Grandpa taught us how to work, all while making us think we were having a vacation. Grandpa did what needed done—easy or not—and we benefited from his sacrifice.

That's what love does.

One of My Favorite Things

I CAN'T WAIT FOR NOVEMBER 4, 2014! It is, after all one of my favorite things in life. On that day, I get to go stand in line, receive a ballot, duck into my private little booth—how exciting is that—and have my say.

The thing is, I'm not just looking forward to November 4th because of the present dissatisfaction with the direction of America. I am excited because this is something that I was raised to deem important. In my family, voting was never questioned.

Turning eighteen wasn't a rite of passage in our family because we could move out but because we could now vote.

I was taught that we vote because we are American; it's as simple as that. After all, it's our right and our responsibility.

The right to vote is an important part of our freedom. It is a gift, and we are responsible for taking care of that gift. I watched my grandparents and parents get excited about voting. They paid attention to the news. They discussed politics. Then, they made the best decision they could and voted.

I remember a conversation between Grandpa Jones and my dad. Grandpa was nearing the end of his life and was concerned about the direction of the country. He hoped to leave a better place for his grandchildren. Had he done enough to ensure that? He was born in 1905 and saw hard times, lived through good government and bad, and voted a lot. But he still felt the weight of responsibility. Overheard conversations like that make an impression.

When Ronald Reagan died, I sat on the couch and cried while I watched the news coverage. My niece sat with me and watched. I could tell she didn't understand what Aunt Miriam was so sad about. "Ronald Reagan was the first president I ever voted for," I explained. "He was a real American hero."

Even at her young age, she understood. Her parents believe in voting too, you see. Now my nieces and nephews, several in their teens, are eagerly awaiting the day they can vote.

It doesn't matter if you are rich, poor, black, white, red, brown, or yellow. You can be unemployed or the CEO of a large corporation. If you are an American and eighteen, you can vote. Why wouldn't you?

A Fresh Start - New Every Morning

"Our dad didn't teach us to give up just because it is hard."

~ Daddy

I LIKE TO TELL PEOPLE that I learned everything I need to know in life from my parents and grandparents. Through their example, I learned how to deal with almost any situation, opportunity, or trial.

I've started a project of interviewing some of my dad's generation for the family newsletter. On his seventy-eighth birthday, I interviewed Daddy, himself. As he was talking, I realized that even this penchant of mine for collecting the family stories came from my parents and grandparents. He told of Grandpa Jones sitting by his mother-in-law in her later years, asking questions and listening. This was the same Grandpa who wrote the story of his life.

These grandparents didn't have easy lives. They didn't come from rich families. They struggled. In fact, one phrase Daddy said has been ringing in my ears this morning. "When Dad and Mom went broke there in the Sandhills, they had to move out of the hills and rent places." Imagine being forced to move away from the land you loved because your cattle were suddenly worthless. When all you have is a sod house, and you lose even that—that's tough!

On the promise of a milk cow and a place to live in exchange for breaking horses, they moved down to southern Nebraska and lived hand to mouth. Eventually—moving place to place—they worked their way out of the hole. When they retired in 1983, they moved to town with enough money to live frugally for the rest of their lives. Grandma was ninety-seven when she died, and her money paid for her room at the nursing home almost clear to the end.

They demonstrated that with faith in God, hard work, and perseverance, we can finish life well.

I remembered this when I experienced a disappointment. The publishing company to which I sent a manuscript rejected it. I wasn't shocked, but I was disappointed. No one likes rejection, even when it is offered with constructive criticism. I had a little pity party, but then I started thinking about my grandparents. What would they say?

Grandpa McKnight would give me a big bear hug and say, "We are so very proud of you, Susie. We are thankful for the way you are using your talents to serve Jesus."

Grandma McKnight taught me a verse that came to mind. "I will lift up mine eyes unto the hills, from whence cometh my help. My help cometh from the Lord."

Grandpa Onstott would echo this sentiment and tell me that God is sovereign, all-mighty, all-knowing, and in control, and I should do my best and leave the results to Him.

Grandma Jones would say, "Well." Then after a moment of silence, she would ask, "What are you going to do with it now?"

Grandpa Jones taught us not to give up just because it is hard.

There you have it. I don't need to feel rejected, because I have

God-given talents. I need to remember whose project this is (God's) and who holds the power (God) and do my best. I need to put this behind me and persevere. I need to move forward.

So, I'll hold the memories of the things they taught me close to my heart and—like they did—with faith, hard work, and perseverance, I'll accomplish what God wants me to accomplish.

Why Do I Do This?

For I know the thoughts that I think toward you, saith the LORD,
thoughts of peace, and not of evil, to give you an expected end.

~ Jeremiah 29:11

Great is Thy faithfulness,

Great is Thy faithfulness.

Morning by morning new mercies I see.

All I have needed Thy hand hath provided;

Great is Thy faithfulness, Lord, unto me.

~ Thomas O. Chisholm

THERE ARE DAYS WHEN I wonder why on earth I am doing
this. What made me think I could be an author? What is it that
pushes me ahead, motivating me to keep on going in the face of
discouragement?

There are several reasons, probably some I don't even recognize, but here
are the three biggies.

First—*God.* I am coming to realize more all the time how much
God has been and is guiding the events of my life. The things I have
accomplished, the places I have been, the dreams that have been ful-
filled, and even those that have been unfulfilled are all orchestrated

by God. I can see it—sometimes as it is happening—and always after the fact. Like the phrase in the song "Great Is Thy Faithfulness" that says, "All I have needed Thy hand hath provided," God has given me everything I need to do what He wants. God made me who I am. I am a teller of stories. I am a fixer. I like to take care of people. I want to help people do better. This writing and speaking is a gift from God. But even more, it is a responsibility. I believe this is something I am supposed to do. Therefore, I must do it.

A second reason is the people who have gone before me. They were my inspiration. Their story-telling captured my mind. Their love and faithfulness led me to desire to tell their stories. They and their stories must not be forgotten. I am proud of my heritage, and I want everyone to know how special my grandparents and parents were and are! I want others to benefit from the legacy of life lessons they left me. If we don't learn from the wisdom of the ones who have gone before, we are doomed to make unnecessary and hurtful mistakes.

The final reason involves the people who are coming after. I don't understand why God chose not to give us children of our own here on earth, but God does all things well. He doesn't make mistakes. I do know that I treasure the children in my life all the more. I am not childless. I just borrow other people's children. My nieces and nephews are the smartest, most beautiful children I know. They make me laugh. They inspire me. Sometimes they make me cry. They look up to me—incredible. I come alive when I am with them. They give me more than I could ever give them. My goal has been to teach them the things they will need to be successful in life. Unfortunately, sometimes it seems like the things they remember aren't the ones I intended—things like eating ketchup with pinto beans is really yummy, or throwing spaghetti on the ceiling to see if it will stick is a good way to test if it's done—but I'm hoping that along with those fun things they will remember the more important life lessons. Lessons like "right feelings follow right actions," and "you can choose your actions, but not your consequences." And the most important one—bring Aunt Miriam chocolate when she is old and in the nursing home. Just kidding . . . kind of . . .

So there you have it. Why do I write?

I write because I want to glorify God by being who He made me to be.

I write to remember and to help others remember those who have gone before us.

I write so the children will know the truth that they can accomplish whatever dreams God puts in their hearts.

I write to leave a legacy. A legacy for life.

Bruce's "Two Cents' Worth"

IN THE LAST FEW YEARS, Miriam and I have been increasingly aware of the legacies we have received from our "families." I put that word in quotes because there are times where the legacy comes from or through people who are not related by either blood or legalities but by affection or friendship. In my case it's even multi-generational.

Like Miriam, I had multiple sets of grandmas and grandpas. But in my case it was not because of death and remarriage but, as the song says, "the bonds of love." My extra grandparents are honorary-adopted.

When my mother was a young woman in North Carolina, she became good friends with Doris, a young woman from Florida. When Doris was making a trip home, Mama went with her. Doris's family "adopted" Mama—to the extent that I grew up with an honorary set of grandparents. That set of relationships has lasted for more than sixty years now and has spanned two more generations. Mama spent a good portion of the last several years of her life with Lily, Doris's sister-in-law, and because Mama passed away not long before Miriam and I met, Miriam got to pick Lily as her "mother-in-law."

That may have conditioned me to repeat the process when I was working just outside Chicago. One of my coworkers invited me to a holiday celebration with her family. It wasn't long until I had a Grandpa Hy and Grandma Babs. After we got married, Miriam very quickly came to love them; she said they reminded her of her own grandparents. The resemblance between Grandpa Hy and her Grandpa McKnight struck her as especially strong. Grandma Babs is the only grandparent either Miriam or I have now, and we go to great lengths to visit her if it's at all possible when we are traveling between the South and South Dakota.

My extra grandparents—and their extended families—enriched my life in countless ways, from the simple and complex "bonds of love" to the recipes that came down (and a few that went "up" or even "sideways"). I hope I (and now we) have returned some of the blessing, especially to the young people to whom I am "Uncle Bruce."

Miriam's mom refers to their "family vine," with its step-, step-step-, and adoptive ties. Mine might be described rather as a "family cloud." With all this complexity, Miriam and I might be forgiven for getting a little confused with each other's family ties, but we're coping quite well, instead savoring the richness of our blessings. We thank God for His generosity in this regard.

Wait Not, Want Not

WHEN I WAS A KID, Mama would sometimes get exasperated with my or my brothers' slowness to make a choice or decision and would say, "Do *something*, even if it's wrong!"

When it comes to preserving your own legacy, the best advice we can give you is not to wait, lest you someday find yourself "in want," having let valuable pieces slip away. And unlike Mama's old admonition, there's hardly a wrong way to do it. These are some of the parts of our legacy and how we preserve them.

RECIPES AND FAVORITE FOODS

The twin senses of smell and taste are the most powerful triggers of memories. We've all had those moments when a smell or taste has put us into a veritable time warp and taken us, for just a flash, back to a time and place long gone.

The best way to preserve these is, of course, to practice them and use and celebrate them. My mother was an exceptionally good cook and seldom used formal recipes. She made biscuits by the way the dough felt as she worked it with her fingers. I never learned that from her, so I can't make a decent biscuit at all, much less any as good as hers. But I do have some of her recipes, and if I want to try to recreate something just the way she used to do it, I call my brothers and we try to figure it out. We all learned to cook—a necessary life skill, guys, and not just for girls!—and we can usually either remember how she did things or figure it out. The key parts, though, are practicing the skills and talking about them, both of which are ways to rehearse and remember.

Miriam has mentioned earlier putting together their family cookbook. She told you only part of how much fun they had and didn't dwell at all on how much work it was, but it's easier now than it used to be, with all of us already storing so much on our computers and sharing so much online. That family cookbook has become one of the strongest ties in their whole family, I think. They're always pulling out and using recipes from aunts or cousins, and every one of them is tied to countless memories and associations.

The wonderful thing is that with computer storage being virtually unlimited these days, this kind of thing can just keep growing as they and younger family members add to the trove. And database programs allow all kinds of additional documents such as stories, pictures, and even sound and video files to be associated with recipes. The old "family cookbook" can be a huge storehouse of multimedia experiences if you want it to be. It can even be the gateway to your whole archive. What richness! But it would take somebody with better focus than we have to just go in and pull out the one or few needed recipes and not get sidetracked.

PICTURES

A better term might be "visual artifacts," since pictures can now include not just the cardboard rectangles with images on them but also all the hundreds (thousands? soon to be millions?) of digital images most of us have on our computers. This includes scans of those old pieces of cardboard. (I am now expected, even *required*, to take our portable scanner to the Jones reunions after doing a high resolution scan of a little old picture from the 1930s and finding Miriam's dad being held in his mother's arms when we "blew it up." Nobody knew that was part of the image until then.) For old sepia-toned images as well as other images, it may be useful to make multiple scans, both in color and in grayscale, and at several resolutions, so that the maximum amount of detail is preserved. You may not have a second chance to scan some things. And, finally, scanning can be a time-consuming process, especially if it's also a learning process, so you may want to start early and plan to have a significant amount of time for this activity.

Don't forget other documents. We have scanned old letters and even an example of calligraphy at the Jones Reunion, but any document that will safely fit in a scanner is a candidate. Be careful about old books. It would be better to use a camera and take a photograph than to "break" the spine of an old book by trying to force it flat onto a scanner. A hand scanner that processes a strip at a time might be good for books, but those are not common anymore, and they take practice to get good results.

Organization: Let me give a few cautions about file names. Choose a file name AND a file location on your computer ("folder" or directory) that will let you find your scan or your photograph later. For these purposes, I use both filenames and directory names that begin with the date (in year-month-day format so that it will automatically sort in chronological order), followed by some description. My directory name might be

2012-08-25 Jones Reunion Saturday, or

20120825 Jones Reunion Saturday, or even

120825 Jones Reunion Sat

The filename for scans OR pictures should be descriptive, such as

2012 Jones Reunion ####

where the camera or computer assigns sequential numbers during the scanning process or file upload from the camera or other device. An additional advantage of using chronological names is that these images will automatically display in chronological order when used in slide shows. This makes a "This Was Your Life" kind of show very easy to organize. Directory and file names cannot contain certain characters; trying to set up your dates with a slash, as in 10/25, will give you an error message. And using month-day-year dates will probably make it harder to find your files later – but it's your computer (or file cabinet), and you need to do what works for you.

Equipment: Scanners have become very common as part of all-in-one printers. Our favorite, though, is a small stand-alone scanner that draws its power through the USB connector. It gives good results and is easy to transport and use. Its only drawback is that it's somewhat slow.

I'll discuss archive issues and strategies later.

STORIES

Bare-bones facts and figures like marriage and birth certificates, land and property documents, and wills and probate records give basic structure to any genealogical endeavor. But it's the stories by, from, and about our families that give flesh, color, and *life* to our legacies. For example, Daddy's old shotgun isn't worth much as an antique. But the story that it was bought for his tenth birthday, the only birthday for which he got any kind of birthday cake (a gingerbread man), has given rise to our family's custom of every child getting a gingerbread man on his or her tenth birthday. Because it's unusual, it's also special.

How are such stories to be preserved and passed down? The first and most traditional way is, obviously, telling them—as often as necessary, even to the point that listeners groan when they recognize the beginning of the story. That means they know it, remember it, and will be able to tell it themselves.

Stories have been preserved in sound recordings for over a hundred years. We are fortunate that the equipment for making such recordings is now smaller, less expensive, and more widely available than ever. For example, smartphones are nearly ubiquitous, and one obvious application for those takes advantage of the microphone that is already necessary for the telephone function and uses it to record sounds to the phone's memory. Sound recordings use less memory than video recordings and are easier to obtain. Not only do you not have to worry about lighting and setting and all the other things that go into good video recordings, but because a sound recorder is less obvious, people are likely to be less self-conscious. In fact, a recorder lying peacefully on the table in the middle of a group will often be completely forgotten and ignored, which means that the recorded stories will be in their most natural form. Dedicated digital sound recorders are available and are usually much smaller (and cheaper) than smartphones, but I have not had good luck with them. Older technologies like tape recorders still work and are therefore still useful. However, it is not only getting more difficult to find supplies for them (tapes or cassettes), but those recordings are less stable over time than digital ones can be. (Archive considerations will be discussed later.) A less obvious method of recording sound and video is directly to the computer. Almost all laptop computers and most desktop systems have microphones and/or cameras ("webcams") either built-in or readily available as inexpensive accessories. In order to use these devices, you need to use the appropriate program along with the hardware. It is important to learn how to use it before you need it, though. And yes, this is a lesson that we have "learned the hard way." It saves a lot of frustration and makes things go so much more smoothly when it's only a matter of setup and not of learning curve when it comes time to record. Of all these options, the easiest for us to use has been the smartphones. Check your device's specifications and operating parameters to find out how big a file will result from an hour of recording. Then, if you plan for at least 1½ times as much space as you anticipate needing, you should be okay.

I've mentioned video recording above. Over the last thirty years or so, I've had video recorders in several different formats, and I've seen older "movie cameras" that used actual photographic film that had to be sent off and developed. The problem with all of these technologies is that the formats have changed with time and old recordings become inaccessible when their technology breaks. We have orphaned tapes of our wedding that we can neither watch nor consolidate because they are all incompatible with each other and all the playback devices that we had for them are now inoperable. We need to take them somewhere and have them transferred to a digital format before they degrade too much to be useful.

Not only have changing formats made things difficult, but durability is a consideration. I have not had good luck with durability in any of my video recording devices until the latest ones that are completely electronic and digital with no moving parts at all, not even in the optics. That means that "zoom" features are, in fact, simply cropping and expanding the center of the image, but I think the improvement in durability is worthwhile in at least one of my devices. I'm content to keep the good optics and optical zoom capability in my still camera.

So, if sound recording is so much easier, why bother with video? The answer, of course, is that video captures so much more. A good video recording includes good audio and captures almost everything but the smells associated with the experience. Even a bad video recording is often better than a simple audio recording. Sometimes it's a tradeoff, and you choose what will work best with the people and circumstances you have. And sometimes, it's a spur-of-the-moment thing for which nobody is prepared, and you use what you have—which is a main reason smartphones have become so valuable: we almost always have them with us.

Finally, let us not forget the very most traditional method of all for capturing family history: using pen and paper to write our stories. It is perhaps a stretch to think of recording our stories this way now, but sometimes there is still value in doing something slowly. Old documents, though, not only preserve special facets of the past, traces of character or personality reflected in handwriting, or even, maybe, the faint scent of the writer's perfume, but they sometimes present special challenges. Old handwriting, even when done well, sometimes includes quirks that are the result of the writing instrument. A dipped pen may run out of ink at an inopportune time, leaving an important word faded. The point of the pen may have been flexible, and the writer adjusted to accommodate for that. Sometimes, though, deciphering the letters or even the words is not enough. You may have to learn about specialized abbreviations or jargon of the time, just as you would to read a modern document of a specialized type.

Archival Considerations

Protecting the old, distributing the current, preserving into the future

Conservation and archiving are specialized technical disciplines. If you have old documents that you want to preserve, a few considerations will improve your chances of successfully passing them to the next generations.

First, paper, textiles, and leathers deteriorate most rapidly in bright, warm, and moist environments. Therefore, they should last longest when kept cool and dry and in the dark. Paper (or most textiles) that has become brittle with age cannot be rejuvenated or restored to its original strong condition because the natural polymers that make up the fibers have themselves degraded—the chemical bonds have been broken and the damage is on the molecular scale where it cannot be repaired, at least not with current technology. Acid and light are both common culprits in this degradation process, so use acid-free paper or other wrapping materials. Especially valuable and/or fragile documents can be stored in archival quality sleeves or pockets. Polyester film ("Mylar" is one tradename) is a common material for such use, since it can be acid-free and is both strong for protection and clear so that the item can still be read or studied.

Second, think about the mechanics involved. One way to tear paper along a particular line is to crease it and then work the paper back and forth at the crease. This process mechanically fatigues the fibers and, eventually, they break or tear along that line. The reverse of this means that to preserve documents, do NOT crease them (do NOT dog-ear a book to mark your place; use a bookmark, even if it's just a random piece of paper). Similarly, rubbing the face of a document can physically remove the ink or other writing from the surface.

These same considerations apply to pictures, prints, slides, and negatives. They will all be most stable when stored in a cool, dry, dark place. I have read that photographers used to store their slides and negatives in sealed packages in a freezer. Those who use film probably still do that. Digital data preservation is discussed below.

One way to preserve information in documents is to take pictures and preserve those images. We've already discussed scanning of documents. The most important libraries and museums in the world are busy doing exactly this with their oldest and most valuable manuscripts. A side benefit is that these digitized images are being made available online. Our copies of our own historical artifacts can be duplicated and distributed in similar fashion. We commonly burn a CD of all the pictures and scans we make at any reunion and distribute copies to all who ask for them.

That brings us to the preservation of datafiles.

While non-acid ink on good paper can last hundreds, or even thousands, of years under the right conditions, we already know that many of the media that have been used to store digital are not stable for even ten years. I'm thinking particularly of magnetic floppy disks. If you have files stored on floppy disks that you have not tried to access in years, NOW is the time to see if they are still accessible. Of course, you will have to find a computer with a drive that can, at least in theory, read the kind of disk you have. That is why I have one old desktop machine sitting in a back room.

From what I'm able to find, the best estimates are that current writeable or re-writeable CDs can store data for no more than 25 years, and 20 years is more likely. Commercially produced disks like the ones you buy with software, music, and movies may have a longer life span.

Despite advertisements to the contrary, magnetic tapes and tape drives used for backup had serious problems when I was using them in the 1990s. I do not think there is any serious effort to bring those back to consumers' machines.

So, for the consumer or small/home office, what strategy is most likely to preserve important datafiles for an indefinite length of time? Right now (2013), hard drives seem to be the best bet. Hard drives have been getting more reliable at the same time that their capacities have been increasing rapidly. But what about the dreaded "crash"? Yes, that is a serious issue. That's why you have a backup program in place. (You DO back up your files on a regular basis, don't you?) Given the size of the backup task, the only realistic option is to back up the drive, or at least the important datafiles, to another hard drive. The fastest data copy/transfer is to a second drive in the same computer. The most realistic option may be to use an external drive.

In any case, the *only* way to archive datafiles for long-term storage is some sort of backup program and to migrate all important datafiles to new formats and storage media as those replace what we currently use. It makes keeping our old paper documents and photographic prints in cool, dry, dark storage seem less trouble, doesn't it? For the foreseeable future, there are no practical preservation techniques that are superior to simply being careful with our existing documents.

For more information about
Miriam Jones Bradley
&

ALL I HAVE NEEDED—
A LEGACY FOR LIFE
and other books by this author
please visit:

Website: www.doublecousins.net
Email: doublecousins.net@gmail.com
Twitter: @AuthorMiriam
Facebook: www.facebook.com/DoubleCousinsMysteries
Blog: miriamjonesbradley.wordpress.com

For more information about
AMBASSADOR INTERNATIONAL
please visit:

www.ambassador-international.com
@AmbassadorIntl
www.facebook.com/AmbassadorIntl